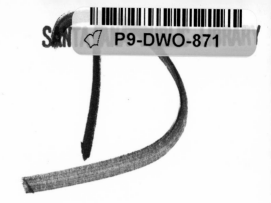

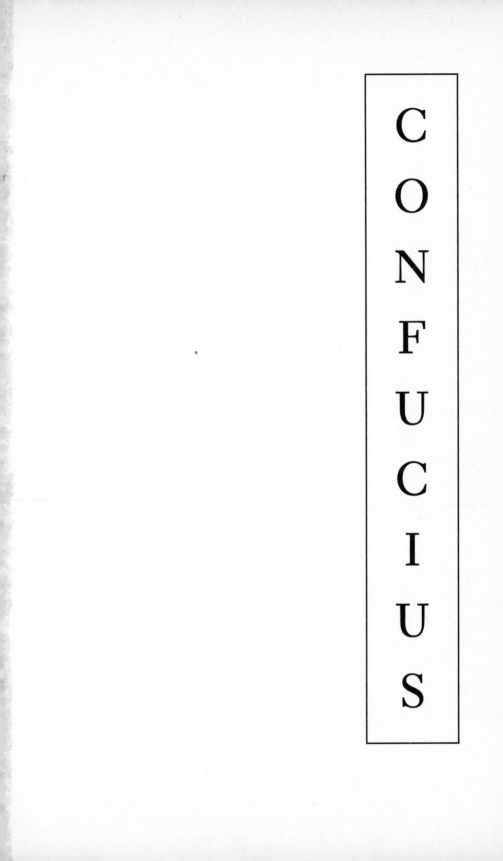

CONFUCIUS

A THRONELESS

KING

MEHER

McARTHUR

CONFUCIUS

PEGASUS BOOKS
NEW YORK

CONFUCIUS

Pegasus Books LLC
80 Broad Street, 5th Floor
New York, NY 10004

Library of Congress Cataloging-in-Publication Data is available.

ISBN: 978-1-60598-117-8

10 9 8 7 6 5 4 3 2 1

Printed in the United States of America
Distributed by W. W. Norton & Company, Inc.
www.pegasusbooks.us

To Roshan

Contents

Acknowledgements

In my exploration of the life of Confucius (or what we understand to be his life), I have been reminded that there are few things more important than treating others with kindness, integrity, loyalty, respect and gratitude. The reminder came not only from his teachings but also from all the people who helped me at various stages of the project.

First, I would like to thank my loyal sister Roshan McArthur for suggesting to me that I could and should write this book. Publishers Tony Morris and Richard Milbank guided me thoughtfully through the initial stages of the proposal and manuscript. As the book progressed, I received valuable advice on structure, approach and content from several scholar-gentlemen, to whom I am deeply grateful. David Schaberg, Ph.D., Co-Director, Center for Chinese Studies and Professor, Asian Languages and Cultures at the University of California, Los Angeles, and Kendall H. Brown, Ph.D., Professor of Art History at California State University, Long Beach, both helped steer me in a better direction with the text. I am particularly indebted to Jonathan B. Markley, Ph.D., Assistant Professor of History at California State University, Fullerton, for taking time out of his busy work and family schedule to read through the manuscript and suggest improvements. His expertise on early Chinese history and culture has brought this book closer to the truth.

I also wish to thank Samuel H. Yamashita, Ph. D., Professor of History at Pomona College, Claremont, Mary Connor, President of the Korean Academy for Educators (KAFE), Thuy Bui, Tom McArthur and Jacqueline Lam McArthur for being kind enough to review specific sections of the manuscripts for accuracy and readability.

Lastly, thanks to my husband, David Marsh, who lovingly devoted hours reading through the manuscript and made invaluable comments that have made it more accessible to the general reader.

I could not have written this book without their help. Any inaccuracies or errors, though, are my responsibility alone.

Meher McArthur
February 2010

Preface

'It is impossible to write a biography of Confucius.'

So a scholar of Chinese history advised me when I started writing this book. His words were somewhat discouraging because I knew he was right. It is impossible to write a standard biography of this important historical figure, mainly because much of his life is (and will no doubt always remain) a mystery.

Confucius lived 2,500 years ago – around the same time as the Buddha in India and a little earlier than Socrates in Greece. Even though the Chinese had already developed an advanced writing system by this time, and stored their important texts in early scroll-like books made of bound wood and bamboo slips, no texts by Confucius or contemporary biographies of him have survived. For centuries, biographers and historians believed that a number of China's great classics were written by Confucius, so information about him and his philosophy was drawn from these scripts and their commentaries. However, *The Analects* (*Lunyu*), the most famous work associated with him, is a compilation of his teachings created by later generations of his followers at least a hundred years after he died. The various classical texts, including *The Book of Songs/Odes* (*Shijing*), *The Book of History* (*Shujing*) and the Lu state history called *The Spring and Autumn Annals* (*Chunqiu*), were long credited to him, but scholars now generally agree that he was not their author – possibly only an editor or commentator. In fact, we do not know if Confucius ever wrote anything down at all about his beliefs or his life. Like other great teachers of the same period, including Socrates and the Buddha, Confucius *talked* to his students. His teachings were passed on orally, so his actual words, and much of his life story, are lost.

Unfortunately, what we know of the life and philosophy of Confucius has been gathered from the accounts of his later followers and from later historians, who themselves often drew from his followers' accounts; and these accounts have turned out to be largely unreliable. Some of the best-known commentaries were written by later disciples such as Mencius (in Chinese Mozi, *c.* 372–289 BC) and Xunzi (*c.* 312–230 BC), who lived several generations after Confucius and had no direct contact with the philosopher or his immediate circle. Their works are therefore interpretations of interpretations, and they generally explain his principles in accordance with their own philosophical beliefs, while romanticising his life to create an exaggerated image of their great mentor. The other early sources of information on Confucius are the records of historians such as Sima Qian of the Han dynasty (206 BC–AD 220), whose writings glorify the Great Teacher as a cultural hero and fill in any gaps in his life story with fanciful tales that extol his immense virtue. This is no surprise when we understand that the rulers of Han dynasty China came to embrace the philosophy of Confucius as the foundation of their political system.

Until recently, most works about Confucius have been based on such early commentaries and histories. But the more that scholars of Confucius, from China and other countries, delve into the existing material about his life, the clearer it becomes that much of his traditional biography is legend and very little is fact, and we are left with many more questions than answers. Did he really save his Duke Ding from ambush by the Duke of Qi? Why did he give up his position as Minister of Justice and go into self-imposed exile? How many disciples did he have? Did he really divorce his wife? As if peeling away the outer layers of an onion one by one, we are coming to dismiss more and more stories about him as untrue, leaving us with very little to feed on as we attempt to understand the real Confucius.

With such scant reliable information available, what is a modern biographer of Confucius to do? When my colleague said that writing a biography of Confucius is impossible, he was not suggesting that I give up on the project. He was merely advising me that I would not be able to write a standard biography of Confucius, that is to say, an account of his life based on facts. Most modern Western studies of him have relied heavily on the earlier Chinese biographies and histories, and so have generally embellished his life with legend and historical inaccuracies. Of the recent English-language accounts, *Confucius: A Biography* by Jonathan Clements (Stroud: Sutton Publishing, 2004) is one of the most enjoyable reads since it paints a wonderful portrait of the philosopher, but it accepts the traditional account of his life without making many attempts to distinguish fact from legend. In contrast, *The Authentic Confucius: A Life of Thought and Politics*, by Annping Chin (New York: Scribner, 2007), aims to dispel some of the major myths and present an authentic account of his life and teachings. The author, a Yale professor of Chinese history and philosophy, chooses to concentrate on some key fragments of Confucius' life because they 'offer more than sufficient grounds and footing to discover him'.[1] With this goal in mind, she begins her book when Confucius was fifty-four years old and leaves out much of the colourful (often legendary) material that has traditionally filled in the gaps between the scraps of more reliable information. Although her account is certainly a valuable resource, it may not be the best place for a beginner wishing to read about Confucius.

Once I had overcome my initial angst about how to tackle this biography, I took the advice of several friends and colleagues and opted to tell a version of the traditional, semi-mythical account of Confucius' life with as few gaps as possible because, even though much of this conventional biography is questionable, it has helped to form an image of Confucius that has endured for centuries in China and nearby cultures. At the same time, however, I do not want to tell a story that is not true! So, while recounting what has generally been believed about his life, I have also attempted to point out as unobtrusively as possible which parts of this story are likely to be untrue. Much of my study is based on the biography written by Siam Qian in his famous text *Records of the Historian*, which, though it tells a great tale and has been the source of many later biographies, is very problematic. So in my version, whenever I run into a major historical inaccuracy – such as the supposed meeting between Confucius and the legendary Daoist sage Laozi, and Confucius' authorship of *The Book of Songs* and the other classical texts – I point out the implausibility of the claims. I reserve my comments on more minor factual issues for the chapter notes. As far as the magical elements are concerned, for example the appearance of dragons at Confucius' birth, I assume that readers will be able to judge for themselves whether or not this could really have happened. The result lies, I hope, somewhere between a good story and a good biography. Although it may not relate a completely accurate account of the details of Confucius' life, at least it gives the reader a sense of his place in his world, his interactions with others and his motivations for developing his philosophy.

Alongside the larger problems associated with writing a

biography of Confucius, there are some other smaller, but also important, issues that should be mentioned here, in particular the use of certain English words to represent the Chinese names for key Confucian concepts. Two words in particular, *ren* and *junzi*, are critical to the understanding of Confucius' thinking, yet problematic to translate. The term *ren* refers to a concern for the welfare of others. Typically rendered into English as 'benevolence' but also as 'humanity', 'humaneness' or 'compassion', *ren* is the very centrepiece of Confucius' teachings, as it is this important quality that permits strong, balanced and meaningful relationships, within the family and at all levels of society. I prefer to translate *ren* as 'benevolence', which literally means 'to wish well', and seems closest to Confucius' belief that we want for others what we wish for ourselves, his version of the Golden Rule. However, on many occasions, particularly when I am quoting from *The Analects*, I use the term 'humanity', in accordance with the translator.[2] The second critical word is *junzi*, which I have chosen to render as 'gentleman'. *Junzi* literally means 'son of a lord' and originally denoted a man of social superiority. However, because Confucius repeatedly employed the term to refer to a man of advanced virtue, *junzi* took on a new meaning, which gradually gained popularity during his time. To him a *junzi* was a morally superior man, someone who walked a virtuous path armed with great intellectual knowledge as well as deep compassion towards other people. The term is often translated as 'superior man', 'ideal man' or 'great man', all of which imply a high moral status, but to me, 'gentleman', the most common translation, fits well because it too signifies a man of high social standing and one of superior moral virtue.

Finally I think it is worth pointing out that, over the centuries, rulers, including Chinese emperors and Japanese samurai lords, philosophers and educators throughout East Asia and even Western philosophers have generally construed the life and teachings of Confucius in a manner that has suited their own agendas. Some have cited his emphasis on loyalty to one's leader and adherence to one's social status to maintain a strict social order, while others praised Confucius' love of learning and promoted education among the population. Later East Asian philosophers interpreted and reinterpreted his teachings in numerous novel ways, often blending them with other philosophies to create new versions of Confucianism that suited the needs of their own place and time. Families throughout East Asia have emphasised respect and obedience towards parents and elders, and the importance of a good, solid education for each new generation. In all of these efforts, Confucius has been held up as symbol of morality and learning and, as such, his own life story has also been emblematic of the heroic, often selfless effort that is necessary to bring positive change to the world.

It is my hope that this biography will be informative to the growing number of Westerners who have become interested in China and in the historical figure who undoubtedly played the greatest role in shaping this fascinating and increasingly important culture.

INTRODUCTION

China's Great Sage

Who was Confucius?

Confucius was the most influential person in Chinese history. He was a teacher and philosopher who lived in the state of Lu (in modern Shandong province) during the Eastern Zhou dynasty (770–221 BC), a period of intense political turmoil and civil unrest in the area that is now China. He was an avid scholar of Chinese traditional culture, particularly of the history, literature, music and rituals of the earlier Western Zhou dynasty (1050–770 BC), an earlier golden age when rulers were generally benevolent and subjects were contented and law-abiding. Based on his research into the past and his own observations of the present, he developed a philosophy that emphasised compassion and respect at all levels of society and promoted education as a means to develop the mind and cultivate the character. He hoped that a ruler would adopt his approach to social and political morality and interpersonal behaviour and use it to spread harmony and peace.

His teachings attracted a significant number of pupils but were largely ignored by the country's rulers, and so were not applied during his lifetime. After his death, however, his principles were kept alive by his disciples. Within a few centuries his philosophy, which later became known as 'Confucianism', was adopted by China's rulers. This philosophy became the foundation for Chinese government, education and social structure; for more than 2,000 years it has penetrated so deeply into Chinese culture that every Chinese person is familiar with Kongzi, or 'Master Kong', as Confucius is known in Chinese. Even beyond China his impact has been enormous. Versions of his philosophy also spread throughout East Asia, profoundly influencing the cultures of Korea, Vietnam and Japan. Wherever Chinese communities have settled – in Southeast Asia, Europe, North and South America – the teachings of Confucius have always followed. In fact, when we consider the historical and geographical importance of China over the centuries and at the present time, and we take into account the large percentage of the global population that is Chinese, we begin to understand the extent to which the world has felt the influence of Confucius over the last two millennia. Only a handful of people have made such a mark.

Yet despite the importance and fame of Confucius and his teachings within China and overseas, we know very little about the man himself and the events of his life. None of his writings have been preserved and no contemporary biographical records have survived. What we know about his life is drawn from later biographies written by people who did not know him, and what we know about his teachings comes from texts written by students of his students of his students. The lack of factual details, however, has not prevented the teacher-sage and his philosophy from enjoying considerable popularity over the centuries. Indeed, it is perhaps because of this absence of solid information that individuals and governments alike have been able to construct personae for him that have best suited their own personal needs and political agendas. Confucius and his beliefs have represented so many things to so many people over the centuries: he has been a teacher, a gentleman, a god and a symbol of many aspects of Chinese culture. As well as asking '*Who* was Confucius?', we should also ask '*What* was Confucius?' Below are some of the most significant ways that Confucius has been perceived over the centuries in China and beyond – some definitions of 'Confucius', as it were.

THE GREAT SAGE AND TEACHER

Although Confucius did not succeed as a political adviser during his lifetime, he was certainly highly successful as a teacher, as was demonstrated by the loyalty of his students and their attempt to carry on his lessons after his death. What he emphasised to his pupils more than anything else – even over proper moral conduct and adherence to correct rituals – was the importance of study. It was through study, he believed, that his students could develop their minds and characters, both of which were important for professional success, the cultivation of morality and an understanding of ritual. His own life was enriched not only by the study of the great Chinese classics and other ancient and contemporary texts, but also by his interactions with people; he famously believed there were very few people from whom he himself could not learn something. By transmitting what he had learned and experienced to his students, he hoped to enrich them intellectually and spiritually.

In the 2,500 years since his death, Confucius has been regarded in China and beyond as the quintessential wise teacher of ancient times. For some time he was even credited with the writing of China's major classical texts, which have long been at the core of the country's education system. This perception of Confucius was given official backing on several occasions. For example, in the year AD 492, Confucius was granted the posthumous title 'Accomplished

Sage' and later, in 1645, the Qing dynasty Emperor Shunzhi (r. 1644–61) proclaimed Confucius to be the 'Ancient Teacher, Illustrious and Accomplished, the Perfect Sage'. This accolade was particularly meaningful because Shunzhi was not Chinese but a Manchu; by acknowledging Confucius as the 'Perfect Sage' he sought to reassure the conquered Han Chinese people that their new rulers had no plans to change the existing philosophy of the land. Throughout East Asia and beyond, the image of the elderly Confucius as a white-bearded sage leaning on a gnarled staff and carrying a scroll has long symbolised superior wisdom and the supreme importance of education. The Great Teacher has left a profound mark on the people of East Asia, who place a higher value on education than perhaps any other cultural group.

THE ULTIMATE GENTLEMAN SCHOLAR

In his teachings, Confucius emphasised the concept of the *junzi* – an ideal man or gentleman who was superior because of his great moral calibre. The gentleman, according to Confucius, practised benevolence and followed rituals that included honouring his ancestors. He was also highly educated, with a solid grounding in the classics and a sound knowledge of calligraphy, poetry, painting and music. Such an outstanding man could influence others, just as the wind caused the grass to sway and bend. Confucius made it his personal goal to become such a gentleman, but often lamented that he had not yet achieved that aim. However, during his lifetime he was undoubtedly considered to be a *junzi* by his students, many of whom followed him loyally as he wandered around the country, hoping to become gentlemen themselves.

Since his death, Confucius has widely been perceived as the quintessential gentleman scholar, a man of great learning who generously shared his knowledge with others, and a man of remarkable integrity who refused to compromise his values and become corrupted by the world around him. By the eleventh century AD his legendary erudition and moral superiority earned him the posthumous rank of emperor, and eventually even emperors were required to show him respect, for example by dismounting from their horses to honour him when they entered Confucian temples. Over the centuries many Chinese and other East Asians have attempted to emulate Confucius and live as gentleman scholars, studying the Chinese classics, including *The Analects*, and learning the four so-called 'gentlemanly pursuits' of painting, calligraphy, poetry and music, in the hope not simply of educating their minds, but also of cultivating their characters to achieve his high moral stature.

THE GOD OF LEARNING

Confucianism is considered to be more a socio-political philosophy than a religion, and Confucius himself famously did not speak of gods, the afterlife or anything supernatural. However, throughout history there have been those who have chosen to worship Confucius as a deity, specifically a god of learning or knowledge. As early as the second century BC, Han dynasty emperors offered animal sacrifices at the tomb of Confucius. By the fifth century AD, Confucius became the object of veneration in dedicated state Confucian temples throughout the country and many young scholars and their families prayed to him for academic success, particularly in the career-making civil service examinations. The Confucius Temple in Qufu, the town of his birth and death, was built on the site of Confucius' home shortly after he died, and has become a place of pilgrimage for many of his followers for centuries. Confucian temples have also been established in Japan, Korea, Vietnam,

Indonesia and Malaysia. In Hanoi, the Confucian temple known as Van Mieu, or Temple of Literature (built in AD 1070), housed statues of Confucius and his main disciples, to whom offerings were made, and Vietnam's first university was established within its grounds.

Figures of Confucius, often depicted as a bearded teacher wearing courtly robes, seated and holding an official tablet, were sculpted out of stone and bronze and placed in temples as objects of worship. Similarly, devotional paintings, prints and rubbings of carved stone images of the Great Sage were produced and widely circulated. The most famous was that of Wu Daozi (680–740), a Tang dynasty artist, who created the iconic portrait of Confucius as an elderly scholar standing with his hands together as if teaching. Over the centuries more portraits of Confucius and his disciples were created to help promote his ideals and they were used widely in personal worship. By the eighteenth century, worship of Confucius was so pervasive that in 1715 Pope Clement XI considered it a threat to the spread of Christianity in China, and despite the efforts of Jesuit missionaries in China to convince him that Confucian rituals were civil rituals compatible with Christian beliefs, the Pope forbade Chinese Catholics to perform rites to honour Confucius or their own ancestors.

Today, a visitor to the Confucius Temple in Qufu will see hundreds of visitors lighting incense, praying to Confucius, or writing out their prayers on wooden votive plaques that are hung as offerings outside the main hall of the temple. On a visit there in 2008 I witnessed a man performing an intense walking prayer, in which he prostrated himself every few steps and bowed his head to Confucius. When I was leaving the temple complex two hours later, he was still making his way slowly and humbly towards the inner main hall.

A STAMP OF POLITICAL LEGITIMACY

Since the Han dynasty (206 BC–AD 220), although Confucianism was often eclipsed by the popularity of Daoism and Buddhism, many Chinese rulers incorporated the teachings of Confucius into their government policies. His insistence on the importance of virtuous rulers led many emperors to try to appear benevolent, for instance by going down among their people following a natural disaster, and his belief in education for all men led to the formation of a civil service comprising many men of lower social rank but considerable dedication and talent. From around the twelfth century Confucianism experienced a renaissance, triumphing over both Buddhist and Daoist teachings to become the official philosophy once again. This new form of Confucianism, later known as Neo-Confucianism, incorporated elements of Daoism (including the *Dao* and *yin-yang*) and Buddhism (such as discussions of the soul) and implied a parallel between social and political order and a greater cosmic order. Rulers from this period onwards often believed that by espousing Confucianism, they were not only ensuring social and political order in their realm but also preserving the stability of the universe.

Over the centuries, periods of political and economic success in China were often attributed to such Confucian approaches, and each new dynastic regime, even those of foreign rulers such as the Mongols or Manchus, generally followed the same policies. In other East Asian countries, too, rulers adopted Chinese Neo-Confucianist government policies as a means of legitimising their own rule. In Japan in the early 1600s, for example, the Tokugawa Shogunate, or military government, was impressed by the political and economic might of Ming dynasty China and assumed Neo-Confucian ideals to strengthen their control over the populace. In particular, the

Shogunate borrowed Confucius' belief in devotion to one's lord to bolster the existing samurai ethic of loyalty, and it also enforced a rigid social hierarchy which placed the samurai at the top, followed by farmers, artisans and, lastly, merchants. Citing Chinese Neo-Confucian doctrine, the Tokugawa government claimed that only by adhering to this structure and these values could both social and universal order be maintained. This system remained in place in Japan for over 250 years, until it was challenged by supporters of the Japanese emperor who opposed the military government and sought a return to traditional Japanese-style imperial rule.

A SYMBOL OF ANCIENT WAYS

Although numerous rulers in China and beyond sought to forge a connection with the country's ancient past by espousing and propagating the teachings of Confucius, there have been several important Chinese rulers who considered them harmful or antiquated and banned them outright. One of the most notable examples was China's first emperor Qin Shi Huang (259–210 BC), who succeeded, after much bloody warfare, in uniting all the warring states of China under his rule. A follower of the Zhou dynasty Legalist philosophy, which claimed that social order could only be maintained by imposing strict laws and rules upon the people, he outlawed Confucianism and other Zhou philosophies, considering them potentially threatening to his new world order. To prevent the common people from having access to Confucian teachings and using them to challenge government decisions, he ordered the destruction of Confucian books and put to death many followers of Confucius. Some copies were retained in the imperial library for official use, but these books were in turn destroyed when the capital was burned during the collapse of the Qin. (It was only after the fall of the brief

Qin dynasty that Confucianism began to become a powerful force in Chinese government.)

More recently, during the Cultural Revolution of Mao Zedong, Confucius was again demonised. Mao declared him to be a symbol of China's imperial and feudal past and thus an enemy of the people and of their Revolution. Mao criticised Confucius' belief in the importance of a hierarchical social structure as particularly counter-revolutionary, even though he himself borrowed the Confucian concept of loyalty to one's ruler to garner popular support and further his own political aims. Under Mao, texts such as *The Analects*, which contained Confucius' principal teachings, were banned, and Confucian scholars were punished and often tortured. Confucian temples were either turned into museums and libraries or were destroyed, and statues of Confucius inside them defaced.

A SYMBOL OF CHINESE CULTURE

In the last years of the twentieth century, as China began to depart from many of its Communist policies and reinvent itself as a powerful economic and cultural force in the world, Confucius was gradually brought back from political exile and is now being touted as a symbol of the greatness of China's ancient civilisation. After the considerable cultural devastation of the Communist Revolution, the Chinese have sought to rediscover their own heritage, and many have turned to the teachings of Confucius as a means of reconnecting with it.

In 2004 the first Confucius Institute, a public, non-profit organisation run by the Chinese government, was opened in Seoul. The Confucius Institute promotes Chinese culture and language and supports local Chinese language-teaching programmes, following the models of such institutions as the British Council, the Goethe

Institute or Japan Foundation. There are now over 300 such Confucius Institutes worldwide, mostly in universities, and the Chinese government plans to open 1,000 Confucius Institutes by 2020. It is also significant that in 2008, when the whole world was watching the Beijing Olympics, the spectacular opening ceremony began with the first words from *The Analects* of Confucius, which welcome friends from afar. Only a few decades after Confucius was declared an enemy of the Chinese people and the Communist Revolution, the Chinese government is now upholding him as the great symbol of Chinese culture.

Among the Chinese people, too, Confucius has enjoyed a new lease of life. In 2006 a female professor of media studies, Yu Dan, rose to national stardom with her hugely popular television series and best-selling book that interprets Confucius' teachings for modern life in China. Selling roughly ten million copies (six million pirated!) in its first year, the book has been powerful evidence that the Chinese are again interested in what their most famous philosopher has to say about society, politics, education and the human condition.

What did he teach?

No writings by Confucius have survived, but after his death his followers compiled his doctrines in a text called *The Analects*, a collection of sayings attributed to Confucius and observations by his students of his actions, behaviour and dialogues with them. The volume is short and its twenty chapters are assembled in a rather haphazard way, so it cannot be considered a thorough or comprehensive guide to his beliefs. Many of the verses begin with the words, 'The Master said', while some verses contain the teachings of his followers, so the text is very much an interpretation of his work by later students of his philosophy. Yet in *The Analects* we do gain a sense of his priorities and attitudes.

We learn that Confucius was primarily concerned with the human condition. His teachings did not address the afterlife or spirits, and he did not give his views on 'the nature of things and the Way of Heaven'.[1] Instead, he advised his students to keep ghosts and gods at a distance,[2] and focus on people. At the core of his beliefs is the concept of *ren*, or benevolence, a virtue that each individual should strive to acquire, from the most powerful ruler to the poorest farmer supporting his family. An ideal man (his doctrines rarely referred to women) was a *junzi*, a gentleman who possessed this virtue and who behaved with kindness and wisdom towards others. Such a man was also well educated in classical literature, history, music and, most importantly, rituals, particularly those rituals that honoured the family ancestors. Confucius believed that an education in these areas was crucial not only for the development of the intellect but also for the cultivation of the character, and he repeatedly stressed the importance of learning.

The education of the mind and the cultivation of the character were, he believed, the key to creating successful relationships at all levels of society. To him, relationships were the very foundation of society: ruler–subject, father–child, husband–wife, older sibling–younger sibling, and friend–friend. Whatever the connection, both parties were expected to behave according to their status – the person in the higher position with kindness towards the lower and the lower with loyalty to the higher. If such reciprocity was demonstrated, social and political harmony could be achieved. Confucius saw it as the responsibility of the ruler of a state to set the example for his people, by showing kindness towards them and integrity in his political affairs. A leader who faltered in this had no right to rule the people, and should be removed from power.

Although we will never know exactly what he taught his many students, *The Analects* do give us a good guide to his basic philosophy. The following is a closer look at some of the main elements of his teachings. I have included excerpts from *The Analects* that, I believe, best illustrate what his students understood to be his views on these important aspects.

REN

At the very centre of Confucius' teachings is the concept of *ren* – what is perhaps best described as a deep and sincere concern for the welfare of others. *Ren* is a quality that is hard to define precisely, and although the term is mentioned often in *The Analects* and is a crucial concept in his teachings, Confucius did not provide a solid definition of the word as he understood it.[3] In fact, at one point in the text we learn that the Master seldom spoke of *ren*,[4] and on the occasions when he did, he sometimes seemed to contradict himself. For example, on the one hand, he claimed, *ren* could only be achieved with a great deal of work: 'A good man's trials bear fruit – this is goodness indeed',[5] while on the other he suggested that all one had to do was wish for it and it would appear: 'Is goodness out of reach? As soon as I long for goodness, goodness is at hand.'[6] Such seemingly opposing statements can be confusing, and, not surprisingly, the term acquired a mystical quality and has been a subject of debate among Confucian scholars and philosophers for centuries. Translators have struggled to express the concept in foreign languages, and in English it has been rendered variously as benevolence, humanity, compassion, goodness and even love.

To Confucius, *ren* was what he most passionately sought to cultivate in himself. Whoever truly loves *ren*, he declared, would put nothing above it.[7] His whole philosophy, or Way, revolved around the pursuit of this quality, and he urged his students to join him in this quest. To him, true compassion for others, or humanity, is not merely an essential quality for living within society. It is the only true path to individual happiness. Once in possession of it, he told his students, 'even though you only have coarse grain for food, water for drink, and your bent arm for a pillow, you may still be happy'.[8] He also claimed, 'a good [ren] man rests in his humanity [ren], a wise man profits from his humanity [ren]'.[9] In contrast, a man who does not possess ren 'cannot long bear adversity and cannot long know joy'.[10] Indeed, he challenged, 'if a gentleman forsakes humanity [ren], how can he make a name for himself? Never for a moment does a gentleman part from humanity [ren]; he clings to it through trials, he clings to it through tribulations'.[11]

Confucius seems to have believed that the pursuit of ren was not an easy task. This was not a quality that one was born with, but was learned through much hard work and discipline. It could take a lifetime of self-cultivation to develop ren, and to be able to use it naturally. So, when he suggested that a person could just wish for ren and it would be there, he was not contradicting himself. Rather, he was likely implying that once this quality was truly learned, it could be summoned immediately, without much effort.[12] However, even if a student succeeded in acquiring ren, his spiritual quest would not necessarily be over, since this wonderful quality brings with it great responsibility. A student of his Way (Dao), he said, must be strong, 'for his burden is heavy, and his journey is long. His burden is humanity [ren]: is this not heavy? His journey only ends with death: is this not long'?[13] He might also have to make the ultimate sacrifice: 'There are instances where he will give his life in order to fulfil his humanity'.[14] Someone in possession of ren would make such a sacrifice without a second thought, since there was nothing more important in life than showing genuine compassion for others. Only by doing this, Confucius believed, could one be truly human and attain true happiness.

LI

According to Confucius' teachings, one of the most important and effective ways to cultivate *ren* was to study and carefully follow *li*. This word, like *ren*, has a broad meaning and is not easy to translate precisely, but the English terms most often used are 'ritual' or 'propriety'. *Li* applies to such everyday social acts as basic greetings. How we address the various members of our social world – family friends, teachers, employers or government officials – depends on our own social position as we travel through life. We learn our greeting rituals and practise them, sometimes more successfully than others. (In fact, we are mostly unaware that we are performing a rite at all, unless something goes wrong with the encounter and a person is offended.) *Li* also applies to the more elaborate rituals that we perform, such as weddings, graduation ceremonies and funerals. In China, from before the time of Confucius, the most important rite of all was the honouring of one's deceased family members, both during the funeral and afterwards as an ancestor spirit at the family altar.

To Confucius, the point of most social rituals was to help guide people in their day-to-day dealings with others. Rituals provide a means of showing gratitude, congratulations or condolences in ways that can form and strengthen relationships and help people to express needs, wishes and feelings appropriately. 'Without ritual,' he explained, 'courtesy is tiresome, prudence is timid; without ritual, bravery is quarrelsome; without ritual, frankness is hurtful.'[15] With the tools and the structures provided by our social rituals, he believed, people can display such qualities as bravery or frankness in ways that do not hurt or offend others. However, Confucius warned his students to beware of putting form above substance. He insisted that more important than the simple act of carrying out a particular rite was to do so with a sincere heart and with respect, not only towards others, but also towards the act itself. Without this attitude, the ritual would have no real meaning and would be ineffective both as a means of developing good relationships and as a way of cultivating the self.

For example, when it comes to serving one's parents, he taught, 'It is the attitude that matters. If young people merely offer their services when there's work to do, or let their elders drink when there is wine and food, how could this ever pass as filial piety?'[16] Far more important than the gesture of helping others and serving them food and drink was the feeling of wanting to perform this act for them, out of love rather than mere obligation. He despaired that, too often, people carried out so-called filial acts towards their parents without any true emotional connection with them. 'Nowadays,' he lamented, 'people think they are dutiful sons when they feed their parents. Yet they also feed their dogs and horses. Unless there is respect, where is the difference?'[17] The same approach should apply to the more elaborate rituals. When asked, 'What is the root of ritual?', Confucius answered, 'Big question! In ceremonies, prefer simplicity to lavishness; in funerals, prefer grief to formality.'[18] To him, it was much more important to focus on the human aspect of the ceremony itself – for example, the honouring of a family member – than on its form, even if that meant forgoing some of the prescribed details. He further stressed this point by declaring, 'If I do not sacrifice with all my heart, I might as well not sacrifice.'[19]

We can see from these statements that Confucius believed that *li* and *ren* were profoundly interconnected. Performing rituals was an important way of developing *ren*, but at the same time he said that in order to carry out rituals in a meaningful way, they had to be done with sincerity and respect towards others, qualities very close to *ren*. He went so far as to claim, 'If a man has no humanity, what can he have to do with ritual?'[20] So, rituals (*li*) were necessary for the cultivation of compassion and humanity (*ren*), but without this compassion it would be impossible to perform rituals correctly. (For this author, one way of understanding the critical connection between *li* and *ren* is to think of a tightrope walker. Without balance, he cannot walk on the rope safely, but to develop his sense of balance he needs to practise walking on a tightrope – since the act forces him to focus on balance. It seems to me that Confucius saw the correct performance of rituals as a way of summoning up the compassion inside oneself, and that the more one practised using this quality, the more present it will be in one's character and life.)

EDUCATION

'Those who have innate knowledge are the highest. Next come those who acquire knowledge through learning. Next again come those who learn through the trials of life. Lowest are the common people who go through the trials of life without learning anything.'[21]

Confucius did not assume that he had innate knowledge. He undoubtedly ranked himself among the second category of people on his list. He spent his entire life studying in order to understand the world and better himself, believing that learning was an ongoing process and one which would help him develop his mind and his character. He once compared the procedure to the building of a mound: 'If you stop before the last basket of earth, it remains forever unfinished. It is like the filling of a ditch: once you have tipped in the first basket, you only need to carry on in order to progress.'[22] His own studies were in history, literature, traditional rituals and song, particularly those of the Western Zhou (1050–770 BC), a time when he judged the country to have been ruled by wise and benevolent kings and administrators. He felt that much of the wisdom of this period had been lost, and this was why the country was in disarray. He believed that by studying and discussing the various records of the Western Zhou, the rulers of his day could learn how to win the respect of their people and restore peace and stability to their realm; by reading the literature and learning the songs and poetry, people would acquire wisdom about how society worked at a happier time in the country's history. And, by studying and relearning the many rituals and performing them the correct way – with respect and sincerity – people at all levels of society could improve their relationships.

To Confucius, education was less an exercise for the mind than for the spirit. By expanding one's intellect, one would also cultivate one's character. This, to Confucius, was the main goal of learning, but in his day the concept seemed to have been forgotten. 'In the olden days, people studied to improve themselves. Now', he lamented, 'they study in order to impress others.'[23] As a teacher, he delighted in sharing his own knowledge with keen young minds, even those who could not afford to pay. For him the desire to learn and improve one's character was of prime importance: 'I enlighten only the enthusiastic; I guide only the fervent.'[24] Over the years, he took on hundreds of students from all walks of life and shared with them the classics of literature, history, music and ritual. He particularly stressed the importance of studying and performing traditional rituals as a means of developing their moral characters. 'A gentleman enlarges his learning through literature and restrains himself with ritual; therefore he is not likely to go wrong.'[25] This attitude towards education was enthusiastically accepted by his disciples, some of whom became teachers themselves and passed on this philosophy to their own students. Others went on to work in government positions, eventually incorporating this approach into the government's educational programme. However, Confucius lamented that he was unable to convince the rulers of his time that the words and deeds of wise people from days gone by could help them to fix the ills that were plaguing the land.

JUNZI

The Analects is full of references to a type of man known in Chinese as a *junzi* – a gentleman, ideal man, great man or moral man. To Confucius, a *junzi* was not only educated in the classics, but had also mastered rituals (*li*) and had acquired and practised compassion (*ren*) towards others. To become a *junzi* was the ultimate goal of Confucius and his followers. The highest moral and spiritual level a human being could attain, *junzi* were very rare, and although it seems that Confucius' own followers regarded him as such a man, he felt he never attained that level. However, according to *The Analects* he seems to have had a clear understanding of what a *junzi* should be and described him in many different ways. For example, 'A gentleman is proud without being aggressive, sociable but not partisan.'[26] He is 'principled but not rigid'.[27] 'A gentleman is without grief and without fear ... His conscience is without reproach. Why should he grieve, what should he fear?'[28] 'A gentleman takes justice as his basis, enacts it in conformity with the ritual, expounds it with modesty, and through good faith, brings it to fruition. This is how a gentleman proceeds.'[29]

For a gentleman, integrity was more important than wealth or rank, a point that Confucius stressed to his students constantly.

'Riches and rank are what every man craves; yet, if the only way to obtain them goes against his principles, he should desist from such a pursuit.'[30] A *junzi* recognises that true wealth is the successful cultivation of the self by following a path of morality and compassion. 'A gentleman seeks the Way, he does not seek a living. Plough the fields and perchance you may go hungry. Apply yourself to learning and perchance you may yet make a career. A gentleman worries whether he will find the Way, he does not worry that he may remain poor.'[31] Furthermore, the concerns of a *junzi* extend far beyond his own needs and desires. He always cares about others. 'As for the good man: what he wishes to achieve for himself, he helps others to achieve; what he wishes to obtain for himself, he enables others to obtain – the ability to take one's own aspirations as a guide is the recipe for goodness.'[32]

The subject of the *junzi* seems to have been at the centre of many discussions between Confucius and his students. As well as making simple descriptive statements about the character of a *junzi*, the Master also occasionally chose to contrast the *junzi* with a lesser man, or *xiaoren* (literally a 'small man', but also sometimes translated as a 'petty man' or 'vulgar man'). For example, 'A gentleman reaches up. A vulgar man reaches down.'[33] Or, 'A gentleman makes demands on himself; a vulgar man makes demands on others.'[34] He also claimed that 'A gentleman considers what is just; a small man considers what is expedient',[35] and that 'a gentleman considers the whole rather than the parts. The small man considers the parts rather than the whole.'[36] To Confucius the *junzi*, unlike less morally developed individuals, was able to reach upwards and outwards to something larger than himself, enabling him to give freely without demanding of others.

Although such descriptions of the attitudes of a *junzi* were undoubtedly helpful for Confucius' students, it seems that they were also curious about a *junzi*'s feelings and how he might manage them. For example, one student, Zigong, asked whether a *junzi* felt hatred, to which Confucius replied, 'Yes. He hates those who dwell on what is hateful in others. He hates those inferiors who slander their superiors. He hates those whose courage is not tempered by civilised manners. He hates the impulsive and the stubborn.'[37] When asked what a gentleman might fear, Confucius explained, 'A gentleman fears three things. He fears the will of Heaven. He fears great men. He fears the words of the saints.'[38] Yet, although Confucius conceded that a gentleman could have feelings such as hatred and fear, there were other urges that he kept under control. He explained, 'A gentleman must guard himself against three dangers. When young, as the energy of the blood is still in turmoil, he should guard against lust. In his maturity, as the energy of the blood is at its full, he should guard against rage. In old age, as the energy of the blood is on the wane, he should guard against rapacity.'[39] According to Confucius' teachings, a *junzi* mastered all these powerful emotions using *li*. By learning and practising certain rituals, he would cultivate his character so that lust, rage and rapacity could be kept at bay. Ideally, his own self-control would set an example to others around him, and they too would learn how to master their aggressive emotions. 'Through self-cultivation, he achieves dignity ... Through self-cultivation, he spreads his peace to his neighbors ... Through self-cultivation, he spreads his peace to all the people.'[40]

RELATIONSHIPS

To Confucius, the whole point of cultivating one's compassion and morality was to be able to enjoy successful and meaningful relationships with other human beings and thus contribute to a more harmonious society. He rejected the practice of mystics and hermits, who retreated from society in order to develop their characters. 'One cannot associate with birds and beasts,' he said. 'With whom should I keep company, if not with my own kind?'[41] There was nothing more important to Confucius than the way in which people relate to each other at all levels of society and in all aspects of life. His most faithful student, Zilu, summed up his attitude to human relationships beautifully: 'It is not right to withdraw from public life. One cannot ignore the difference between age and youth, and even less the mutual obligations between prince and subject. One cannot discard the most essential human relationships, simply to preserve one's purity.'[42]

Confucius believed that human relationships were the very foundation of society. At the very heart of humanity was the relationship between a parent and a child, and if this relationship was conducted well, others should follow. Early in *The Analects* comes his statement, 'At home, a young man must respect his parents; abroad he must respect his elders,'[43] which is echoed and reinforced by that of his follower, You Rou: 'To respect parents and elders is the root of humanity.'[44] Filial piety is a central precept in the teachings of Confucius and is an aspect of Confucianism that has been given considerable attention over the centuries in many cultures. However, it is important to note that although Confucius believed that loyalty and obedience towards one's parents, ancestors and elders were of great importance, he also held that a parent or elder had a responsibility to be kind and nurturing towards the child or younger person. There should be reciprocity in this and any other relationship. Indeed, when asked by his student Zigong, 'Is there a single word that could guide one's entire life', he answered, 'Should it not be *reciprocity*? What you do not wish for yourself, do not do to others.'[45] To Confucius, therefore, a relationship was a two-way process, in which both parties had mutual responsibilities and benefits. His version of the Golden Rule applied to relationships at all levels of society, and both parties were expected to behave according to their status – the person in the higher position with kindness towards the lower, and the lower with loyalty towards the higher.

GOVERNMENT

In Confucius' day, the kings of the Zhou dynasty had lost their power over the various states of the region and the relationship between the states was very turbulent, the larger ones vying with each other for power and territory and smaller ones fearing for their survival. Within each of the states, chaos prevailed as the reigning dukes fought to hold on to their power against both external and internal threats, without paying much heed to the needs of their own people. Confucius believed that it was because many of the rulers and administrators of his day lacked virtue that the region was in such turmoil. These leaders, from the Zhou kings down to the ministers of each of the kingdoms, had lost their way morally and only if they found it again could stability be restored. It was Confucius' goal in life to become an adviser to a duke or prince and help him to rule virtuously so that peace and harmony would prevail in that region and spread to others. Much of his philosophy was formed with this aim in mind, and many sections of *The Analects* contain advice about how to rule well.

Throughout his career he provided dukes and ministers with advice such as 'Raise the straight and set them above the crooked,'[46] 'Guide the officials. Forgive small mistakes. Promote men of talent,'[47] and 'Mobilise the people only at the right times.'[48] However, his most valuable counsel to rulers and administrators was really no different from that which he gave to his students when they sought to improve themselves. When Confucius was asked by the governor of the small district of She about government, the Master said: 'Make the local people happy and attract migrants from afar.'[49] In this statement he was suggesting that a ruler's priority should be his people, and that by demonstrating benevolence, or *ren*, towards them, he would not only make them happy but also draw more people to his state. He also advised, 'If one can govern the country by observing ritual and showing deference, there is no more to be said,'[50] and suggested that a ruler 'lead the people as if performing a great ceremony'.[51] Since a ruler's behaviour impacted on the many thousands of people in his domain, the pursuit of *ren* and the performance of *li* were more critical for him than for an ordinary person. Confucius believed that it should be the goal of every king, prince, duke or minister to be a gentleman, and described the behaviour of Zichan, a prime minister of the state of Zheng, as an example of a gentleman administrator: 'He followed the way of a gentleman in four respects: in his private conduct he was dignified; in serving his master he was respectful; in caring for the people he was generous; in employing the people he was just.'[52] Confucius strongly believed that if a ruler was a true *junzi* in his private and public affairs, his morality would influence all those below him. 'If you desire what is good, the people will be good. The moral power of the gentleman is wind, the moral power of the common man is grass. Under the wind, the grass must bend.'[53]

Just as he emphasised the importance of reciprocity in family relationships, Confucius also stressed its significance in the relations between a ruler and his subjects. He often compared the ruler–subject relationship to that of a parent and child, in which nurturing care and kindness are rewarded with loyalty and piety. When asked by Lord Ji Kangzi, a powerful minister of the state of Lu, 'What should I do in order to make the people respectful, loyal and zealous?' Confucius responded, 'Approach them with dignity and they will be respectful.'[54] He believed that, just as a father earned his son's respect by showing him kindness, he would only earn obedience and loyalty from his people if he showed them compassion and respect. 'What you do not wish for yourself, do not impose on others,'[55] he advised leaders. He expanded on this idea: 'Lead them by political manoeuvres, restrain them with punishments: the people will become cunning and shameless. Lead them by virtue and restrain them with ritual; they will develop a sense of shame and a sense of participation.'[56] According to Confucius, the people should not be expected to be loyal to a cruel and corrupt ruler, and without their loyalty a ruler was bound to fall. 'Without the trust of the people,' he warned, 'no government can stand.'[57] In contrast, 'He who rules by virtue is like the polestar, which remains unmoving in its mansion while all the others revolve respectfully around it.'[58]

What can Confucius offer us today?

Confucius lived in a world that is very different from ours today, but much of the wisdom credited to him is timeless. His advice that we should aim to be more benevolent and respectful in our dealings with others and think of them before ourselves can be applied to all our relationships and undoubtedly enrich our lives. Simple daily rituals, such as smiling or saying hello to strangers, can make the world a more comfortable place, while holding more formal rituals to honour those who came before us can help us cultivate a sense of gratitude and ground ourselves firmly in history. We should see education less as food for our brain or our careers, and more as food for our souls and characters that can transform a lesson in history, literature, art or music into a moment of connection with the greater human experience. Confucius believed that by cultivating compassion, practising rituals and studying the world, people could become more morally aware, *junzi*, and the more such people, especially in positions of power, the more peaceful and harmonious the world would be. All these beliefs surely apply today.

There is much that we can learn from *The Analects* about living more fulfilling lives. For example, the text opens with the lines: 'To learn something and then to put it into practice at the right time: is this not a joy? To have friends coming from afar: is this not a delight? Not to be upset when one's merits are ignored: is this not the mark of a gentleman?'[59] Such seemingly simple advice actually sums up much of what is important in life. We should learn about the world and apply our learning carefully. We should value our loved ones and enjoy their company. And we should not waste time worrying about what other people think of us. If we could follow this advice alone, we might all be much happier. It seems that Confucius was able to practise much of what he preached. In *The Analects* he is said to have described himself as 'the sort of man who, in his enthusiasm, forgets to eat, in his joy forgets to worry, and who ignores the approach of old age'.[60] This self-portrait certainly suggests that Confucius found much pleasure and happiness in his life, despite his failure to put his teachings into practice in government and the many hard years he spent wandering around the country looking for work. Because he believed what he was teaching, he had the strength and resilience not only to overcome the many adversities that he faced but also to inspire others to follow him and learn his philosophy. Although we look back at his life and teachings through the obscurity of time and legend, his story still offers us much to contemplate that is relevant today.

The Bitter Gourd That Is Not Eaten

Almost exactly 2,500 years ago, an elderly teacher and a handful of his most devoted students were stranded in the wilds of China's Henan province, wondering when and where they would find their next meal. Cut off from civilisation by hostile feudal lords, the group had not eaten for a week and their hunger was testing the limits of their mental and physical strength.

For several years now, the Master and his students had been travelling together from state to state, stopping when the Master found employment with a lord or duke and then setting off again when he left the job, usually after he realised that his employer was morally weak, or when fellow government officials sought his dismissal. The Master was now in his late fifties and his inability to find a virtuous ruler to whom he could offer his moral guidance and political advice caused him much frustration and sadness. For his entire life he had studied the wisdom of the ancients, carefully considered their words and ideas and developed a philosophy which, if followed by people at all levels of society, from ruler to subject and from father to son, was guaranteed to restore peace, harmony and happiness to the world. What ruler, he wondered, would not want this to be his legacy?

None during his lifetime, it seemed. Whenever the Master had been assigned a government position he met with resistance from his various employers, none of whom had been prepared to make sacrifices in their lives in order to become a truly benevolent ruler. Rarely was a sovereign willing to give up his life of luxury in order to reduce the burden of taxes upon the poor peasants who worked the land. Many kings were more concerned with expanding their territories than with ensuring their own subjects were fed and clothed. And when the downtrodden people became restless, most rulers simply laid down laws to keep them in their place and prevent them from challenging the regime. What made matters worse was that however hard the people worked, there was no way for any of them to elevate themselves into a position in government in order to bring about change. Power was hereditary, not based on merit, morality or hard work, and those who had influence in all the states where the Master had been employed were less interested in cultivating their characters and helping others than in enhancing their own status. Not surprisingly, they had little time for his ideas and suggestions, and instead had plotted against him, forcing him to give up his post and search for work elsewhere.

With these people ruling the states, no wonder the world was in chaos. If only a virtuous ruler like the early kings of Zhou were alive today, the Master thought. Such leaders were not only virtuous themselves, but sought and encouraged virtue in others and surrounded themselves with virtuous advisers. With someone like them as his employer, he would have been able to put his ideas to the test, advising his lord to feed the poor, to hire the hard-working and accomplished and even to follow the sacred ceremonies performed to honour his ancestors – something that most rulers today also tended to neglect. His lord would surely restore peace and stability to his kingdom, and soon his example would be followed by other leaders until the world became peaceful and harmonious again.

But, alas, such a ruler was nowhere to be found, and the Master was beginning to realise that he could die without ever seeing his teachings applied in government. This thought had occurred to him for the first time a year or so earlier, when it looked as if the Duke of Wei might hire him as his counsellor. Though the Duke had shown him great courtesy and hospitality, he had not actually offered him a post. This was not the first time he had been overlooked in this manner. He lamented to his students that he was like a bitter gourd that is hung but not eaten,[1] a man ripe with ideas that no one wanted to taste. Yet the Great Teacher, convinced of the truth of his teachings, refused to give up his mission to share them with a noble leader who could use them well.

His students, though also sad and bewildered that those in power did not value the advice of their Teacher, respected his decision to heed his inner voice and abandon his posts. They happily followed him in his wanderings, spurred on by a desire to absorb his goodness and become better men themselves, perhaps even *junzi*, or gentlemen. It was surely his virtue and the power of his teachings, they imagined, that had protected him when his life had been threatened – on two occasions. The first was a few years earlier when, in the state of Chen, he had been mistaken for the bandit Yang Hu and imprisoned for several days until his captors realised their mistake and released him. The second was when the evil commander of the cavalry of the state of Song had tried to kill him by felling a tree where he was standing. Miraculously, the Master had escaped unscathed, and had proclaimed that this was a sign that he was destined to complete his mission.

Over the years the students had become accustomed to their peripatetic life, during which time their Master had shared with them so many of his thoughts on compassion, loyalty, power and the importance of study. Inspired by his wisdom and amazed by his resilience, they were convinced that one day his teachings would prevail. However, now that they found themselves stranded out in the forest with no sign of help, the fear that they all might starve to death far from civilisation was starting to turn devotion into despair. Zilu, one of the most passionate of all the pupils, could not understand why his Master remained calm and serene when they could all die of starvation. Why wasn't his Master upset by their current situation? He cried out at him in anger, 'Is it right that a gentleman should be reduced to such dire straits?'[2]

The Master responded, 'The wise man may indeed find himself in distressing circumstances. But in such a situation, only an ordinary man is thrown off balance.'

Zilu was embarrassed by his outburst since it demonstrated that he still had much to learn from his teacher.

His Master immediately saw an opportunity to turn an awkward moment into a lesson for his students and drew, as he often did, on the words of the ancients. He asked Zilu, 'The *Shujing* says: "We are not tigers or rhinoceroses that we should remain in desert places." So why am I in such a position?'

Zilu replied, 'In my opinion, it is because our goodness is not sufficient to cause men to believe us; it is because our wisdom is not sufficient that men do not follow our precepts.'

His Master shook his head and then went on to give Zilu examples of several great heroes from ancient times who had met with bitter ends, despite their goodness and wisdom. He then asked the student Zigong the same question. His reply was, 'Your wisdom is so great that there is no one in the empire who will accept you. Master, you should lower the level of your teachings a little.'

To this the Master countered, 'A good farmer sows, but is not sure that he will reap. A skilful artisan is not sure that he will please. The gentleman puts wisdom into practice and upholds basic rules and principles, but has no assurance that he will win acceptance. If you say that in order to gain acceptance, one must not practise wisdom, your aspirations are not very high.'

Then the Master posed the original question to his favourite student, Yan Hui, who responded, 'Your wisdom is most lofty; that is why there is no one in the empire who will accept it. However, if we do not practise wisdom, we should be ashamed, and when, having practised it, we are not employed, it is the lords who should be ashamed.'

The Master was delighted with this last answer and joked with Yan Hui, 'If you were a rich man, I would like to be your overseer!' By this, he was probably suggesting that Yan Hui not only understood the importance of virtue but also possessed it himself, so that if he were to own riches too, he would be just the sort of benevolent ruler the Master would like to serve.

This type of exchange was the reason the students remained with their Master, even though they risked losing their lives. Despite any fear that the Master might be experiencing, he was able to share with them a profoundly important lesson and even colour it with a touch of humour and irony that made it all the more digestible. Despite his own sense of failure as a political adviser and the image of the bitter gourd that hovered in his mind, he could still believe in himself and his mission. And despite his compassion towards them in their shared dire predicament, he was not going to be soft on them now and allow them to forget that losing their integrity would be a far greater tragedy than losing their lives.

The Master was not destined to die in the wilds of Henan that year, nor were his students. He lived another fifteen years but, to his great regret, was never able to put his teachings into practice in government. Indeed, the image of the bitter gourd, hanging on a vine without ever being eaten, stayed with him until his death. However, his students made sure that his life's work was not in vain and passed on his teachings to their children and their students, gradually sweetening the gourd so that it was not only devoured hungrily by their rulers, but its seeds bore fruit that has been the philosophical and moral staple for millions of people in China and beyond for centuries.

China at the Time of Confucius

When Confucius lived (551–479 BC), there was no such country as China. The area that we now know as China, or Zhongguo (meaning 'central country') in Chinese, was a patchwork of states embroiled in conflict with each other for power and territory. Much of this vast area was unified under the Zhou dynasty during the first part of their reign, which is known as the Western Zhou period (1050–770 BC), because their capital was located in north-western China (near modern Xi'an in Shaanxi province); but by the eighth century BC the dynasty had lost all political and military might in the region. During the Eastern Zhou period (770–221 BC), when Confucius lived, the Zhou kings only held nominal control over a small domain centred on their new capital city, Luoyang, which was situated to the east in modern Henan province. There was no centralised government keeping peace and order in the region, and all around the capital a number of largely autonomous states ruled by feudal lords vied for supremacy with their neighbours, while also struggling to contain continuous political conflicts within their own borders.

This unstable political situation was not simply the backdrop for Confucius' life; it became his very reason for being. For many of his years, Confucius believed that he was on a Heavenly mission

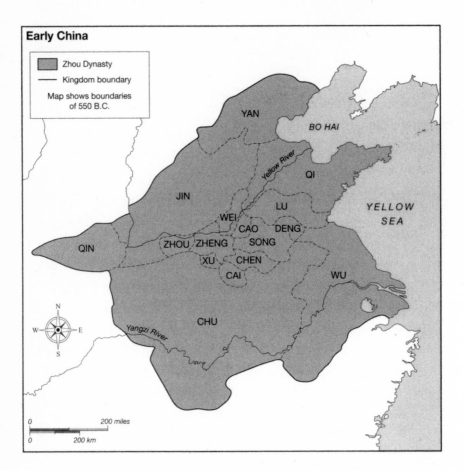

Early China

Zhou Dynasty

Kingdom boundary

Map shows boundaries
of 550 B.C.

YAN

BO HAI

Yellow River

QI

JIN

YELLOW
SEA

WEI

LU

CAO

DENG

ZHOU

ZHENG

SONG

QIN

XU

CHEN

CAI

WU

N

Yangzi River

W   E

CHU

S

0   200 miles

0   200 km

to restore harmony to the region and reunite it under the Zhou kings.[1] He regarded the earlier Western Zhou period as a golden age, when the land was ruled by benevolent kings who were advised by wise and compassionate counsellors. Throughout his life he studied the government, history, rites and literature of the Western Zhou, shared this knowledge with his students, and hoped to use it one day to advise a noble ruler on how to create a harmonious state. For a professional role model he looked to the Duke of Zhou, the brother of King Wu, the first king of the Zhou dynasty. Nearly 600 years earlier the Duke had helped unify and pacify much of the region as a regent to King Wu's son, and then later became a respected political adviser to his nephew when he ascended the throne as King Cheng. Confucius believed passionately that if the rulers of his day followed the ways of the Western Zhou kings, and if they allowed him to advise them in the manner of the Duke of Zhou, then peace and prosperity could return.

When studying Confucius and his teachings, it would seem that he might have been a happier man and a more successful political adviser if he had lived in the 'golden age' of the Western Zhou. Then, he believed, virtuous rulers still existed and honourable advisers like him could find rewarding employment with them. Instead, Confucius lived during the Eastern Zhou period, a time of intense political and social turmoil, and he was never able to find a job with such a ruler, seemingly because there were so few of them. However, it was undoubtedly *because* of this turmoil, rather than *in spite* of it, that the Eastern Zhou dynasty became what is described as one of the most important periods of intellectual and philosophical activity in the history of China. The Western Zhou dynasty was an era of immense cultural growth, but it is generally agreed that it was under the Eastern Zhou dynasty that the intellectual and spiritual foundations of Chinese civilisation were laid.

It was precisely because of the intense conflict in the region that Confucius and other philosophers of the Eastern Zhou age developed theories about social and political harmony. The chaos made their work necessary, and although the instability of the time made it hard for their theories to be put into practice during their lives, their teachings greatly contributed to the stability of later periods in Chinese history.

There are many parallels between political and philosophical developments in Eastern Zhou China and other parts of the world. In fact, this period is often referred to as the 'Chinese Axial Age' and considered part of the global Axial Age, a critical period in world history when some of our greatest spiritual and philosophical thinkers, including Socrates, Jeremiah and the Buddha, responded to the turmoil of their age by posing crucial questions about humanity and spirituality.[2] As in Greece, Western Asia and India at roughly the same time (between 900 and 200 BC), China was increasingly torn apart by violence and warfare, and discussions about morality and justice became more common. With the world around them in chaos, philosophers and spiritual leaders were called upon to provide answers to life's great questions: What causes suffering? How can we achieve peace and harmony? What does it mean to be a virtuous person? What gives our lives meaning? Such questions weighed heavily on the philosophers and teachers of the Axial Age and drove them to develop their doctrines and share them with others. Confucius devoted his life to searching for the answers to such fundamental questions and passing them on to his followers.

The Western Zhou (1050–770 BC): ruling with a Heavenly Mandate

The Zhou dynasty began with great promise and, according to the Zhou rulers, with a Mandate from Heaven (*tianming*). The belief that a king and dynasty can only rule with Heaven's blessing has been one of the most important concepts in Chinese politics, and has provided the foundation for the establishment of many of China's great dynasties. The doctrine is traditionally believed to have been initiated by the Duke of Zhou, who proclaimed it to the people of the new Zhou Empire. The main principle of *tianming* is the notion that, as long as a king is virtuous and undertakes his sacred duties (including performing rituals to honour his ancestors), he will be able to retain his Heavenly Mandate and rule indefinitely. However, if he becomes corrupt or neglects these duties, he will lose Heaven's blessing, a loss that is manifested most clearly in natural disasters such as earthquakes and floods, and in violent uprisings among his people.

According to Zhou texts such as *The Book of History*,[3] from which we glean much of our contemporary information about the period, the preceding Shang dynasty (1600–1046 BC) was in severe decline because their rulers were ineffective at best. The last Shang king, Shang Zhou, was one of the most corrupt and sadistic rulers in Chinese history, and he reputedly imposed high taxes on his people in order to pay for an extravagant lifestyle which included drunken and often violent orgies. Under such a dissolute ruler, unrest spread. The first Zhou kings considered themselves more than justified in supplanting the Shang – they believed that they were mandated by Heaven to do so. In 1050 BC, the Zhou army rose up and overthrew the Shang, succeeding them as rulers of the region. Although the Zhou conquerors employed the concept of the Heavenly Mandate in part to convince the subjects of the conquered Shang of the legitimacy of the new Zhou regime, they undoubtedly believed in their Heaven-appointed role, and the early Zhou rulers seem to have understood that with this blessing came great responsibility.

The first centuries of the Zhou period were a time of relative calm, prosperity and cultural growth. Three Zhou leaders were credited with great virtue and skill in laying the foundations for a stable Zhou state. King Wen, the 'Cultured King', made the initial preparations to overthrow the corrupt Shang court by forming alliances with neighbouring states and tribes to gain their support, but he did not live to participate in the actual offensive. His son King Wu, the 'Military King', then carried out the attack, defeating the Shang at their capital of Yin, near modern Anyang in Henan province. Out of respect for the Shang, King Wu chose not to kill all the members of the royal household, but left a Shang prince as nominal ruler of the capital city so that the prince could continue sacrifices to his family ancestors. King Wu is generally considered to have been a virtuous ruler, but he died only a few years after conquering the Shang. His son was still a child, so his brother, the Duke of Zhou, served as regent for the young king, further extending and consolidating Zhou territory. Once King Wu's son came of age and took over the throne as King Cheng, the Duke stepped down as regent and became the young king's loyal adviser. These three men – King Wen, King Wu and the Duke of Zhou – have long been admired for their wise political decisions, military skills and genuine concern about the well-being of their people. They have also been traditionally credited with establishing new ritual traditions, though recent archaeological research suggests that the Zhou followed Shang ritual traditions for some time.[4] Confucius viewed these benevolent rulers as models for later leaders and believed that their virtue was the key to peace and stability. He spent much of his life searching for a ruler who possessed similar qualities.

Throughout their reign, the Zhou kings bolstered their political power by maintaining a strong connection to the divine, and by following the Shang tradition of calling themselves 'Sons of Heaven'. The Shang kings had gained their religious status and power from the belief that their ancestors were in direct communication with the High God, Shang Di, or Di, who ruled the universe and all the other gods. They conducted rituals to honour the royal ancestors and Shang Di, including offerings of food and drink, and human and animal sacrifices, all with the goal of ensuring that their ancestors would act on their behalf to secure the goodwill of Shang Di. The Shang kings also performed the function of shaman-like mediators between the human and spiritual realms; one way in which they communicated with the spirit world was through divination rituals. They questioned the spirits through inscriptions on oracle bones in the hope of determining the success or failure of a battle, harvest or other important undertaking.

The Zhou shared many of the Shang beliefs, but instead of the god Shang Di their focus was on the concept of Heaven, which they viewed as the sacred moral power of the universe. Since it was this that had granted them their earthly status, the Zhou kings made regular sacrifices to Heaven at the capital, while also conducting rituals to honour their own family ancestors. The Zhou communicated with the spirit world too but they used a new divination system laid out in *The Book of Changes*, or *Yijing* (also known as *I Ching*), a text which interpreted trigrams, or sets of broken and unbroken lines that helped to predict successful harvests, battles and health. Although Confucius is known to have become fascinated with the *Yijing* in his later life, he always placed far more emphasis on honouring parents and ancestors, and he praised the early Zhou rulers for their dedication to their forebears.

During the Western Zhou period, the kings continued to enlarge their empire by leading their powerful armies in the conquest of neighbouring tribes and states. When they were not engaged in territorial expansion, they resided in the twin capitals of Feng and Hao near modern Xi'an. Rather than rule all their lands directly, they used family members and their most trusted lords to govern the more distant areas, typically dispatching these surrogates with troops to establish walled garrisons in the conquered territories. In some regions the king recognised local chiefs as his representatives, granting them power and title in exchange for loyalty, military service and tributes. The Zhou royal family also intermarried with lords of other families, creating a network that enabled them to consolidate their power throughout the region.

In the Western Zhou period, Zhou society was a kin-based tiered aristocratic hierarchy. Below the king were the lords, or regional governors, of the various Zhou territories. These lords owned all the land and granted their subjects land to farm, in a form of enfeoffment that has often been compared with the medieval European feudal system. Known as *fengjian*, it was reputedly introduced by the Duke of Zhou and has been considered one of the dynasty's greatest achievements, since it was designed to be fair towards those who actually worked the soil. Under this system, much of the land was carved up into lots that were in turn divided into nine squares forming the Chinese character '*jing* (#)', meaning 'well'. The grain from the central square was given to the government, who stored it and distributed it to the people in times of famine or bad harvest, while the farmers, who made up a large percentage of the population, lived off the harvest from the remaining eight squares.

In the early years of their reign Zhou rulers demonstrated military ability, strong family ties throughout the country, skill at settling disputes and fairness towards their subjects, all of which earned them the respect and support of the various lords and the loyalty of the populace. The result appears to have been a period of relative stability and prosperity. Confucius had great admiration for such a society, in which people at all levels – from the king to the peasants – behaved well and in a manner that was appropriate to their status. To him, this was the only way that a society could function properly.

With such prosperity, the country also underwent significant technological and cultural growth. Bronze manufacturing, which had already been sophisticated under the Shang, reached new levels of excellence. The military greatly benefited from improved bronze weaponry and horse and chariot fittings, while bronze farming tools and equipment increased agricultural output. The most noteworthy bronze objects of the period were the ritual vessels used by the rulers in their elaborate funerals and then buried with the deceased in the tomb to provide food and drink for the soul in the afterlife. The vessels were decorated with intricate designs of stylised birds and other natural motifs, and were inscribed with increasingly lengthy texts describing family relationships, important accomplishments and the occasion for which the vessels were used.

In the cultural realm, the most significant development was the creation of a sophisticated Chinese writing system that enabled the dissemination and storage of information among a larger proportion of the population. The earliest extant Chinese writing was to be found on the oracle bones of the earlier Shang rulers, but this script only consisted of a few hundred characters and was reserved for use in royal divination practices. During the Western Zhou dynasty many thousands of ideographs were created, and they evolved into characters that are closer in form to those used in China today. Paper was not invented until centuries later, so much of this writing was inscribed in ink onto thin, vertical strips of wood or bamboo that were strung together like a mat and rolled up for storage – the antecedent of the traditional Chinese hand scroll. (It is also very likely that silk was used as a writing surface, but no early examples of texts on silk have survived.) With the evolution of the writing system and the creation of the first 'books', literacy spread throughout the upper classes. Over the course of the Western Zhou period and continuing into the Eastern Zhou period, some of the great classics of Chinese literature were produced, including *The Book of History*, China's earliest narrative text, recording the deeds and sayings of rulers from ancient times until the early Zhou dynasty, *The Book of Songs*, which contains the earliest Chinese poetry, and *The Book of Rites*, which describes ancient rituals, court ceremonies and social forms. These and other Zhou classics were to become the core of Confucius' teachings, as he believed they represented the wisdom of a greater time.

The Eastern Zhou (770–221 BC): a weakening Mandate

Many of the great cultural and economic advances of the Western Zhou period continued into the Eastern Zhou, the age in which Confucius lived. This is often further divided into two distinct subperiods: the Spring and Autumn period (770–475 BC) and the Warring States period (475–221 BC). Cities developed in size and number, and trade increased between them. Archaeological evidence shows that iron was being used by this time, iron tools enhancing the region's agriculture. Silk, which had been produced since the Shang dynasty, was cultivated and widely traded and was not only used as material for clothing the wealthy, but also as a surface for writing and painting. Rolls of silk were even used as currency.

Despite these cultural and economic developments, the Eastern Zhou is generally characterised as an era of immense political instability, triggered by the worsening circumstances of the Zhou court. The Zhou had maintained firm control of the country until the early eighth century BC, when King You (r. 781–771 BC) replaced his queen with a concubine. The queen retaliated by joining forces with non-Chinese Rong tribesmen from the north, killing the king and putting her own son on the throne. To protect themselves from further attacks, the Zhou moved their capital eastwards to Luoyi (near modern-day Luoyang). The new Zhou king, Ping (r. 770–720 BC) ruled a much smaller area and, although from this time onwards Zhou kings still performed a religious role as intermediaries with Heaven, they now reigned alongside a number of other equally or more powerful leaders claiming the title of king. They were never able to regain their former political or military power so, not surprisingly, political chaos ensued.

Without a strong central authority, the region broke down into a loose affiliation of largely autonomous states, some bigger and more powerful than others. During much of Confucius' lifetime the north was dominated by Jin in the centre (modern Shaanxi province) and Yan and Qi towards the east (modern Hebei and Shandong respectively). In the west, Qin took over former Western Zhou territory, and Chu (modern Hubei, Hunan, Chonqing, Henan, Shanghai and parts of Jiangsu) was most powerful in the south. In the early part of the Eastern Zhou period, states generally followed a code of chivalrous conduct that regulated warfare among themselves. For example, one state was not permitted to attack another while it was mourning the loss of its ruler, and a battle could not begin until both sides had time to line up their troops.[5] Despite this sportsmanlike code, however, the rulers were constantly engaged in political manoeuvrings to boost their own strength and avoid being absorbed by larger neighbours. Strategies included building up domestic economic power through trade, strengthening their armies, in particular the cavalry, and forming allegiances with other states, usually by marrying sons and daughters into the ruling families. Far from being virtuous rulers with a Heavenly Mandate who cared for their people, kings and officials clung jealously to power with little regard for their subjects.

Politics in the state of Lu

The chaos throughout the region was echoed within the borders of most of the Zhou states. Confucius was from Lu, which is in north-eastern China in what is now Shandong province. Lu was founded in the tenth century BC after the Duke of Zhou sent his own son there to establish a settlement. This connection to the respected Duke was a source of great pride to the state, and certainly to Confucius, who emphasised the connection in his teachings. Like many other states during the Eastern Zhou period, Lu was politically volatile, facing threats of absorption by larger neighbours states as well as the machinations of several rival families within Lu who were eager to seize control. Lu was bordered to the north by the large and powerful state of Qi, which launched an unsuccessful invasion of Lu in 684 BC and occasionally appeared close to invading again. To the east was Wei and to the south were Song, the state from which Confucius' own ancestors are said originally to have hailed, and Chu was to the south-east. The capital of Lu was the city of Qufu, and it was here that its rulers, vested with the title of 'Duke', maintained their regime with varying degrees of success until they were finally annexed in 256 BC by the state of Chu.

One of the political problems plaguing the Dukes of Lu for much of this period was that of the Three Families, hereditary counsellors to the Duke who were descended from three brothers of a past Duke of Lu. In the mid-seventh century BC, roughly a hundred years before Confucius was born, when the current Duke of Lu was dying his three remaining brothers disagreed on the question of succession. After much intrigue and bloodshed, which included the deaths of the two younger brothers, the eldest brother won. The descendants of all three brothers were granted hereditary status as advisers to the Duke of Lu and were formed into three new families, the Jisuns (descendants of the eldest brother), the Shusuns (those of the middle brother) and the Mengsuns (those of the youngest brother). These three hereditary families did little to empower the Duke. Instead, they repeatedly undermined his power and went so far as to appropriate the state army for their own use, dividing up the soldiers and weapons among themselves and integrating them into their own existing armies.

Over the years, the Three Families gained in power over the Duke while also plotting against each other, creating a highly volatile political climate in Lu. By Confucius' time these Three Families, in particular the Jisun clan, had usurped much of the Duke's power, amassing more financial wealth than the Duke himself, imposing taxes on the people which they kept for themselves, and giving the Duke advice that would only undermine his position further. To Confucius such counsellors, with their lust for power and disregard for their ruler, were the very antithesis of the Duke of Zhou and of himself. With such advisers a king could not rule effectively, the people could never be content, and correct social propriety and structure could not be maintained.

In *The Analects* Confucius declared:

When the world follows the Way, rites, music, and military expeditions are all determined by the Son of Heaven. When the world has lost the Way, rites, music, and military expeditions are all determined by the feudal lords. Once it is the feudal lords who determine these matters, their authority seldom lasts for ten generations; once it is their ministers who determine these matters, their authority seldom lasts for five generations; once the affairs of the country fall into the hands of the stewards of the ministers their authority seldom lasts for three generations. In a world which follows the Way, political initiative does not belong to the ministers; in a world which follows the Way, there is no need for commoners to dispute over politics.[6]

Clearly, the world Confucius was born into had not only lost its way, but had lost the Way, or the *Dao* – the correct path of action which could ensure social harmony. The Zhou Empire was a ghost of its earlier form and the Zhou kings, who were still referred to as 'Sons of Heaven', seemed to have squandered their Heavenly blessing to rule. In their stead, feudal lords ruled over the fragments of their empire, and struggled hard to avoid being replaced in turn by their own ministers, and then by the ministers' stewards. With society so visibly collapsing, it was only natural that by the Eastern Zhou period commoners should become preoccupied with the world of politics, and that some among them should try to effect political change. In the sixth century BC Confucius, the most influential commoner in China's history, studied the rites, music and history and made it his life's goal to help his world find the Way once again.

3

Early Life and Family

Confucius was born in the district of Zou in the state of Lu in 551 BC, to a retired, elderly soldier called Shuliang He[1] and his teenage second wife or concubine, Yan Zhengzai. Before his birth his father already had ten children with his first wife, but nine of them were girls and the tenth was a boy who was crippled in some manner, most likely with a club foot. According to traditional Chinese beliefs, girls were not as valuable as boys because only boys were allowed to perform the traditional rituals to honour the family ancestors. Since their son was disabled, he was unlikely be able to sweep the ancestors' graves or make offerings at their altars, acts that were crucial to ensure the future protection of the family. Without an able-bodied son, Shuliang and his family could face disastrous consequences. Confucius' very conception thus arose from Shuliang's desire to protect his family from such disaster.

From long before Confucius was born, it was important for people at all levels of Chinese society to honour their family ancestors in the afterlife, just as they honoured their parents while they were still alive. This hierarchic principle based on age, in which the young respect the old and the living honour the dead, has been one of the most important and enduring aspects of Chinese society. Not only was it considered a vital means of preserving order and accord in the world of the living, but it also guaranteed a harmonious relationship with the world of the spirits.[2] Even though deceased family members had crossed over into the spirit world, they were still regarded as the heads of the family, and by treating them as such the living family stood to benefit from their spirit powers. It was believed that if the ancestors were honoured properly with the appropriate offerings, sacrifices and rituals, their spirits would enjoy a certain amount of power and influence in the spirit world. This influence would then enable them to assist the living family by interceding on their behalf with other, more powerful spirits including Shang Di, the High God, to affect natural phenomena such as the weather and the annual harvest.

However, if a family did not honour its ancestors, their spirits would not only cease to assist the family from within the spirit world, but they could re-enter the world of the living in the form of vengeful, evil phantoms called *gui* and cause havoc and destruction among their descendants. Terrifying tales of such vindictive *gui* and their wicked deeds have abounded throughout Chinese history and were no doubt familiar to Shuliang and his family. If Shuliang did not produce a son, his family would be at the mercy of *gui* for generations to come. Not surprisingly, Shuliang was determined to father a healthy son.

Shuliang's first wife was no longer capable of bearing more children, so Shuliang looked for a young woman who could provide him with a suitable male heir. Although he was probably close to seventy years old when he approached the neighbouring Yan family, he was successful in persuading them to give him one of their teenage daughters, Zhengzai, as a wife. This was in part due to his past reputation as an heroic soldier. Shuliang had served in the military with distinction, once saving a squad of soldiers during a siege on an enemy castle; they had rushed in through an apparently unguarded gate, but they soon realised that they had fallen into a trap. As the enemy started to lower the portcullis to cut off their retreat, Shuliang, a man of great height and strength even in his fifties, grabbed the heavy gate and held it up long enough for all the men to escape. For his strength and bravery in this famous achievement and others, he received many accolades and honours. A marriage to such a man, even in his senior years, would be considered respectable, and Zhengzai's family, who were of modest means and reputation, would benefit from the alliance.

Furthermore, although Shuliang was not a man of great wealth and status, he could claim to be of royal stock. His family, the Kong, were descended from a long line of scholars with an aristocratic lineage that could be traced back to the Shang dynasty. After the defeat of the Shang by the Zhou in 1050 BC, one of the king's sons had refused to fight and withdrew from court. The Zhou rulers chose to spare his life and gave him the state of Song, just south of Lu, in south-central China (modern Henan province) to rule. From there, he was to continue making sacrifices to the ancestors of the defeated Shang dynasty, an apparently generous gesture on the part of the Zhou. In fact, the conquerors probably hoped that these offerings would prevent the vengeful spirits of the Shang ancestors from rising up against their conquerors. This last Shang prince remained in Song and bore children who, though no longer considered royalty, continued to rule the state as minor aristocrats. After several generations, the prince's great-grandsons had their power stolen from them by an uncle. One of the great-grandsons, Fangzi, fought back, killed the uncle and became the Duke of Song. The other, Fuhe, chose not to fight and renounced his position, losing his claim as a ruler of Song. His descendants were scholars and administrators and by 710 BC, the time of Fuhe's great-great-grandson Jia, they no longer held any rank. At this time, they apparently took the name Kong. Although Jia was an upright man, he was murdered by a minister who coveted his wife, sparking a feud between the two families that lasted several generations. To escape the feud, Jia's great-grandson (and Confucius' great-grandfather) eventually left Song and travelled north to Lu, where both he and his son became civil administrators. By the sixth century BC the Kong family had lost their hereditary titles and privileges, but they had earned a reputation for scholarship, loyalty and pacifism. Confucius' father Shuliang seems to have been the only warrior among them. He did, however, also serve as a district steward, keeping up the Kong family tradition of government service.[3]

It is not clear whether Shuliang and Zhengzai were ever actually married, or whether she simply became his concubine.[4] In China at this time it was already common for men of wealth and status to have a first wife and one or more concubines, or 'er nai', literally, 'second wives'. As in other cultures with similar traditions, this practice was maintained to ensure the birth of a son and heir, thus guaranteeing the continuation of the family line. Generally, the first wife held the highest status, and the second wife or concubine had little power or say within the household. However, if the first wife did not bear a son, her status could be threatened by a concubine who produced a male heir. Such a concubine immediately gained higher rank within the family as the mother of the heir, leading to much wrangling and jealousy among the wives as they tried to maintain their own position. Because of the cost of supporting multiple wives and large numbers of children, it was usually only men of considerable means who could afford this practice. It was typical in the case of China's emperors, and over the centuries some were known to keep hundreds, even thousands, of concubines. Confucius' father, however, was not a rich man. Although he had a certain standing as manager of the district of

Zou, his large family appears to have been a strain on his resources. Before Confucius was born Shuliang already had ten children, and some scholars have suggested that the mother of his disabled son was actually a second wife or concubine,[5] meaning that Confucius' mother may have been a second concubine and that after Confucius was born Shuliang had a total of three women and eleven children to support, quite a burden for a man of his income. It is not clear from records what became of the first two mothers of Shuliang's children, and we know very little about how the various wives and children lived and related to each other, though we can assume that life was not easy for any of them, especially after Shuliang eventually died.

Whatever her status, Zhengzai is said to have been a strong-willed woman, and she was clearly pragmatic too. Although she was surely disappointed to be marrying such an old man, she understood the importance of bearing a son for Shuliang before he died. According to the traditional accounts of her pregnancy, she and Shuliang visited Mount Ni, a sacred hill near their home, and prayed hard for a son. There are many legends that tell of miraculous happenings during the time between this prayer and Confucius' birth, no doubt created by followers to demonstrate his great spiritual power and importance. In one legend, as Zhengzai descended from Mount Ni, all the trees and plants bowed down to her in respect. That same night she is said to have dreamed that Di appeared to her and told her that she would have a son who would become a sage, and that she should give birth to him in a hollow mulberry tree. Soon afterwards, she had another dream in which five elderly men who represented the spirits of the five planets[6] came to her leading a *qilin*, a mythical unicorn-like creature who only appeared when a truly great and virtuous individual was in the world (or about to enter it). The *qilin* knelt before her and cast forth from its mouth a jade tablet bearing an inscription saying that she would give birth to the son of the essence of water and that he would succeed the Zhou dynasty, but as a king without a throne. Zhengzai then tied an embroidered ribbon around the horn of the *qilin*, and the beast disappeared.[7]

Her son was eventually born in the twenty-second year of the reign of Duke Xiang of Lu, or 551 BC.[8] According to the legends, his birth was also a magical event. Following the advice she had been given in her first dream, Zhengzai found a cave in a nearby hill that was known as the 'hollow mulberry tree' and prepared for her labour there. On the night of Confucius' birth, legend tells, two dragons guarded the left and the right of the hill and Heavenly maidens flew above the cave, bathing Zhengzai in perfume. When her son was born, a spring of clear water bubbled up from the cave and, after the boy was bathed in it, dried up again. More legends tell of the baby having various extraordinary physical features, including a mouth like the sea, lips like an ox's and the back of a dragon.[9]

As was common during the Zhou dynasty, Confucius was given two names, a personal name, or *ming*, a sort of affectionate nickname used only by oneself and one's elders, and a 'style' name, or *zi*, which was conferred on males at twenty when they came of age and which was used to address them by adults of the same generation on formal occasions and in writing. His personal name was Qiu, meaning 'mound'. According to the Han dynasty historian Sima Qian, this was because he had a small indentation on his head that resembled a small hill.[10] In addition, his parents had prayed for a son at Mount Ni, or Ni Qiu, so the nickname had a double significance. Because of his position in Shuliang's family he was given the style name of Zhongni, or 'Second Son', although he was to be the only son who mattered in terms of the family line.

So as a child he was known as Kong Qiu, and as a young man he was formally addressed as Kong Zhongni. The name Kong Fuzi or Kongzi was given to him later when he became a respected teacher, both names showing reverence and translating roughly as 'Master Kong'. (The name 'Kong Fuzi' was Latinised as 'Confucius' by Jesuits priests who arrived in China in the late sixteenth century.)

Unfortunately, as a child Confucius does not seem to have enjoyed a very stable family life. It is not clear where his father lived after Confucius was born. He may have remained with his first wife and their children, but it is also possible that he left his first wife to be with the mother of his only healthy son. We do know, however, that when Confucius was only three years old Shuliang died, leaving his mother a young widow and Confucius with little memory of a father. He and his mother lived together in a home that was separate from Shuliang's first family. From some accounts, his other wife and her children were unfriendly to Confucius and his mother, and did not even invite them to Shuliang's funeral, presumably because by producing the male family heir, Zhengzai had diminished the status of the first wife.[11] Although Shuliang was no doubt grateful to Zhengzai for his healthy son, he had not been a wealthy man. After he died, it seems that what little was left of his estate was used for dowries for his nine daughters and for the care of his invalid son.

As a single mother with relatively low status and very little money, Zhengzai did her best to meet her son's needs and worked hard to give him a good education. She made especially sure that he was taught the details of the rituals that he would need to perform to honour his father and the rest of his family ancestors, since carrying out such rites to protect the family had been the very reason for his birth. As a loyal son he would have been expected to prepare offerings of food, drink and incense for the ancestors and to know how, when and where to place the vessels on the family altar. The young Confucius appears to have thoroughly enjoyed learning about these rituals, so much so that when other children played with regular toys, he was said to have pretended to conduct a rite by laying out bowls and cups on a table as if they were offering vessels on an altar.[12] Many of the ceremonies and social forms of the age were later recorded in *The Book of Rites*, a text which became one of the great Confucian classics and which many historians believed that Confucius compiled. Although Confucius was devoted to traditional ritual and protocol from his childhood onwards, it is unlikely that he was the author of this major work.

Another part of his early education was to learn the lyrics and melodies of the traditional songs and hymns that had survived from the earlier part of the Zhou dynasty and before. Many of these songs were about basic human issues, including love, marriage, work and war, and some were hymns reserved for ceremonial occasions.[13] The following verse may have been among the songs that Confucius learned as a child. A type of love divination, the playful verse is reminiscent of the rhyme 'he loves me, he loves me not', and would have appealed to children and adults alike.

Plop Fall the Plums
Plop fall the plums; but there are still seven.
Let those gentlemen that would court me
Come while it is lucky!

Plop fall the plums; but there are still three.
Let any gentleman that would court me
Come before it is too late!

Plop fall the plums, in shallow baskets we lay them.

Any gentleman who would court me
Had better speak while there is time.[14]

Songs such as these were not only instructional about the ways of the world and the roles of different people in society, but they also probably gave comfort and pleasure to the young Confucius and his mother in their impoverished home. His love of traditional songs remained with him throughout his life and, as a teacher, he encouraged children to learn them as he had done, since they 'can provide you with stimulation and with observation, with a capacity for communion and with a vehicle for grief.'[15] This suggests that when he was a child the songs had helped him cope with the many difficulties he faced without money or a father. When he became a teacher, he often cited passages from certain songs to illustrate important points in his lessons to his students, including his own son, and he constantly reminded them that *The Book of Songs* was an essential part of any gentleman's education. In part, these traditional songs and their accompanying music reminded him of an age when society was more harmonious (and so was the music),[16] and on many occasions he is said to have been profoundly moved when hearing them.[17]

It is likely that he learned about rituals and songs from his mother and other family members and friends, and most likely in a home setting. Even though he was poor it is also possible that the young Confucius attended a local school, but there is no reliable information confirming this. One legend tells of his attending a school in the neighbouring state of Qi when he was seven years old, but this would have been unlikely because of the distance and expense required to do so.[18] Most probably, Confucius had a mixture of home schooling and classes with local teachers, perhaps in small, informal classrooms, much like those he himself taught when he was older. Later in his life, according to *The Analects*, Confucius commented on his upbringing and education, implying that they were far from adequate for one with his social aspirations. 'In my youth, I was poor. Therefore, I had to become adept at a variety of lowly skills. Does such versatility befit a gentleman? No it does not.'[19] Because he grew up with little money and no father, he would have had to assist his mother with many practical tasks at home, and by doing so he learned the 'lowly skills' of which he later spoke. These tasks no doubt took him away from his studies, which he would surely have lamented at the time. However, although he apparently considered himself less of a gentleman for possessing such skills, he did not seem to regret the trials of his childhood, since by helping his mother he was being a good, filial son.

Although it is unclear where Confucius received much of his education, we can assume from his famous statement in *The Analects* – 'At fifteen, I set my mind upon learning'[20] – that he was a dedicated student from an early age. He was an avid student of history and read many of the historical texts written during the Zhou dynasty. These books contained records about the major events and personages of the Zhou dynasty and preceding Shang and Xia dynasties. They also included tales of legendary emperors of the predynastic age, such as Yao, a man of great virtue, Shun, who developed agriculture and established an education system, and Yu, who tamed the floods.

One source of these tales was *The Book of History*, a compilation of historical records that probably existed in some form in Confucius' day. Considered the earliest Chinese narrative text, this volume was likely well known to Confucius, and in *The Analects* he refers to it, though not as often as he does to *The Book of Songs* and *The Book of Rites*. The following passage from *The Book of*

History is typical of the type of legend that no doubt fuelled Confucius' imagination and spirit as a young student of history. It describes how Emperor Yu struggled to conquer the Miao, or San Miao, people by force, but finally won them over by demonstrating to them his great virtue:

20 The emperor said, 'Alas! O Yu, there is only the prince of the Miao, who refuses obedience; do you go and correct him.' Yu on this assembled all the princes, and made a speech to the host, saying, 'Ye multitudes, listen all to my orders. Stupid is this prince of [the] Miao, ignorant, erring, and disrespectful. Despiteful and insolent to others, he thinks that all ability and virtue are with himself. A rebel to right, he destroys all the obligations of virtue. Superior men are kept by him in obscurity, and mean men fill all the offices. The people reject and will not protect him. Heaven is sending calamities down upon him. On this account I have assembled you, my multitude of gallant men, and bear the instructions of the emperor to punish his crimes. Do you proceed with united heart and strength, so shall our enterprise be crowned with success.'

21 At the end of three decades, the people of [the] Miao continued rebellious against the emperor's commands, when Yi came to the help of Yu, saying, 'It is virtue which moves Heaven; there is no distance to which it does not reach. Pride brings loss, and humility receives increase: this is the way of Heaven. In the early time of the emperor, when he was living by Mount Li, he went into the fields and daily cried with tears to compassionate Heaven, and to his parents, taking to himself and bearing all guilt and evil. At the same time, with respectful service, he appeared before Gu Sou, looking grave and awe-struck, till Gu also became truly transformed by his example. Entire sincerity moves spiritual beings; how much more will it move this prince of [the] Miao!' Yu did homage to the excellent words and said,

'Yes.' Thereupon he led back his army, having drawn off the troops. The emperor also set about diffusing his accomplishments and virtue more widely. They danced with shields and feathers between the two staircases of the court. In seventy days the prince of Miao came to make his submission.[21]

As a student Confucius probably relished such tales of heroism and bravery, of good vanquishing evil and of virtue conquering all. Although the tales of the ancient rulers were based largely on legend and the stories of the Western Zhou rulers were related from the biased point of view of Zhou historians, they made a strong impression on young Confucius and he carried them with him as he grew older. Later in his life as a teacher, he cited the ancient kings Yao and Shun as rulers of exceptional moral calibre, and often compared the kings and dukes of his own time with more virtuous rulers of days gone by. Because of his love of history and his references to people and events of the past in his teachings, Confucius is closely associated with *The Book of History*, although he was probably not one of its authors or compilers. Along with the other two books, *The Book of Songs* and *The Book of Rites*, *The Book of History* became one of the great Confucian classics and was later considered essential reading for anyone hoping to achieve a position in government.

When Confucius was eighteen or nineteen he married a young woman of the Qiguan family from the state of Song, whence his distant ancestors hailed. Little is known about his wife (including her name!), other than that she bore him a son and two daughters, one of whom died as a child. Not much is known either about their marriage. In fact, the historian Sima Qian does not even mention it in his biography of Confucius. Some sources suggest that it was stormy and ended in divorce when the couple were in their early forties.[22] If their marriage was indeed troubled, this would not be surprising considering his childhood: he grew up without being able closely to observe a husband–wife relationship. Even if his father had lived longer, the age difference between his father and mother would have been unusual and potentially problematic. However, whatever the state of their marriage, it is worth noting that at the Temple of Confucius in Qufu, one of the halls is dedicated to his wife and contains an altar with an ancestor tablet for her. Furthermore, in the section of the temple used by the descendants of Confucius, the main altar is dedicated to him and his wife, so they are revered as a couple, suggesting that their marriage may have been solid.[23]

Having lost his father so young, Confucius probably had no memory of a father–child bond either, and this may have affected his own relationship with his children. From texts, we are provided with very little material about them. We know that around 530 BC his wife bore him a son, which was, of course, of great importance to his family and the continuation of his line. To commemorate the occasion the Duke of Lu sent the family two carp fish, a gesture that suggests that Confucius must have enjoyed some rank and respect in the state of Lu despite his lack of wealth. In thanks, Confucius gave his son the personal name Li, meaning 'carp'. Apparently the boy was known by the nickname Boyu, or 'Top Fish', from the characters Bo meaning eldest brother, and yu meaning fish.[24]

We also know that his son went on to become one of his disciples, though it seems that Boyu was not given special treatment over the others. The following excerpt from The Analects offers us a glimpse of Confucius' relations with his only son:

Chen Ziqin asked Confucius' son: 'Have you received any special teaching from your father?' The other replied: 'No. Once, as he was standing alone, and I was discreetly crossing the courtyard, he asked me, "Have you studied the Poems?" I replied: "No." He said: "If you do not study the Poems, you will not be able to hold your own in any discussion." I withdrew and studied the Poems. Another day, as he was again standing alone and I was discreetly crossing the courtyard, he asked me, "Have you studied the ritual?" I replied "No." He said: "If you do not study the ritual, you will not be able to take your stand in society." I withdrew and studied the ritual. These are the two teachings I received.'

Chen Ziqin went away delighted and said, 'I asked one thing, and learned three. I learned about the Poems, I learned about the ritual, and I learned how a gentleman maintains distance from his son.'[25]

This excerpt suggests that Confucius did not cultivate a warm, loving relationship with his son, preferring to keep him at a distance, more like teacher and student than father and son. Boyu, it seems, was understandably intimidated by his father, and apparently tiptoed around the family home so that Confucius would not notice him. When his father did spot him on these two occasions, he merely urged him to read two of the great classics. Boyu does not comment on whether or not he was pleased with his father's advice, stating simply that this is what he learned from his father. Sadly for Boyu, not only was he treated more as a disciple than as a son, he does not even seem to have been one of Confucius' favourites. Boyu's name is rarely referred to in *The Analects* or other texts, but a number of other disciples, such as Zilu, Zigong and Yan Hui, are mentioned regularly as engaging in stimulating exchanges with Confucius about morality, politics and the like. Confucius was particularly fond of Yan Hui, a young man from a poor family whom Confucius deemed to be of exceptional moral calibre. Over the years, Confucius appears to have become fonder of Yan Hui than of his own son. Because Confucius lived to such a great age (seventy-two or seventy-three), he outlived some of his students and his son. When Boyu died in his late forties *c.* 483 (the year Boyu's son and Confucius' grandson, Zisi, was born), Confucius was presumably saddened; there are no records of his reaction to his son's death. However, when Yan Hui died four years later, Confucius was utterly devastated. According to *The Analects* he wailed wildly, saying, 'Alas! Heaven is destroying me! Heaven is destroying me!' His other disciples were shocked at his behaviour and said to him, 'Master, such grief is not proper.' When they then gave Yan Hui a grand funeral, Confucius lamented, 'Yan Hui treated me as a father, and yet I was not given the chance to treat him as my son,' that is, by giving him a modest funeral, like the one he gave his own son.[26] Confucius died later that same year, perhaps affected by the loss.

We may know very little about Boyu, but it is more than we know about his daughters, a fact that is not surprising considering the traditional Chinese attitude towards women as socially inferior to men. Apparently, Confucius and his wife lost their first daughter when she was still a child, but their second daughter survived. The only reference to her in traditional texts is in *The Analects*, where it was noted that Confucius selected a husband for her, one of his followers, Gongye Chang, also known as Zichang. Gongye Chang, he declared, 'would make a good husband. Although he has been in jail, he was innocent.'[27] It was critical for a woman to marry well, and Confucius would have given the selection of a husband for his daughter careful consideration, so we can assume that this man was of high moral character – perhaps someone who was wrongfully imprisoned for standing up for his beliefs. Other than the fact that she married Gongye Chang, we know nothing about his daughter – not even her name. Confucius, and his disciples and the historians who recorded his life and teachings, no doubt shared the common negative perception of women in China 2,000 years ago, and he and his teachings have been heavily criticised in modern times as being anti-women. Many scholars cite the following excerpt from *The Analects* as evidence of his sexism: 'Women and underlings are especially difficult to handle: be friendly, and they become familiar; be distant, and they resent it.'[28] His defenders, however, counter that although Confucius and his followers may have been guilty of ignoring women, they did not set out to oppress them.[29]

Despite his apparent low regard for women, Confucius does appear to have been deeply reverential towards his own mother, in part from his strong sense of filial piety, an attitude that was already of great importance in this early period of Chinese history.[30] To Confucius, filial piety was the foremost attribute of a gentleman and was essential in the development of one's moral character. In *The Analects* he is said to have taught, 'A gentleman works at the root. Once the root is secured, the Way unfolds. To respect parents and elders is the root of humanity.'[31]

He demonstrated this piety when she died around the year 527 BC, when Confucius was in his mid-twenties. According to tradition, a bereaved son or daughter was required to spend twenty-seven months (extended over three years) in mourning, since this represented three times the gestation period of a baby and was the length of time that children were completely dependent on their parents. Official mourning meant taking time off work, wearing special clothes (made from rough cloth and not silk), abstaining from certain foods (such as fine white rice), refraining from listening to music and, most importantly, performing ceremonies honouring the deceased parent. Confucius felt very strongly about this tradition and criticised others who cut short their mourning period or skipped details of the rituals. Of Zai Yu, one of his disciples, who suggested that one year was enough time to mourn one's parents, Confucius complained, 'Zai Yu is devoid of humanity. After a child is born, for the first three years of his life, he does not leave his parents' bosom. Three years' mourning is a custom that is observed everywhere in the world. Did Zai Yu never enjoy the love of his parents, even for three years?'[32]

Confucius was certainly a pious son but, for him, honouring his deceased mother properly was more than an act of filial piety. It had been his mother who had taught him about rituals and instilled in him the sense of their importance. The least he could do for her in return was to conduct all the mourning rites with the utmost reverence and regard for protocol. He may also have gone beyond what was required of a son when it came to her funeral. It is recorded that although he arranged for an appropriate burial for her, he later exhumed her tomb, found and exhumed his father's tomb (which was presumably with his other family) and buried them together in a new grave site. He erected a mound over their coffins so that he could identify their burial place in later years.[33] The new grave mound is said to have collapsed after a heavy rainstorm, reducing Confucius to tears.[34]

If this legend is true, it is very revealing about his feelings towards his own family circumstances, in particular about the status that he wished his mother had actually held within the Kong family. Perhaps he went this far to show his respect for his mother because he perceived her as a person who had fulfilled all her social roles in a most worthy manner. To Confucius, successfully discharging one's ethical duties was of utmost importance to people of both sexes and all social classes, and he was deeply in awe of men and women who managed to accomplish this.[35] At the various stages of her life his mother was a model daughter, wife and mother. As a daughter, she had obeyed her father and married a man more than three times her age in order to help raise her own family's status. As a wife of an elderly man, she had done her duty to him and swiftly borne a son who could continue his family line. And as a mother, she had provided for her son as best she could without a husband or much money, and she had prepared him well for his role in maintaining the family line. Although there is no specific mention of Confucius' admiration for her in *The Analects* or other texts, he surely viewed her as a highly honourable daughter, wife and mother. It is not surprising, therefore, that her death motivated him to break with protocol one of the few times in his life to alter the family burial arrangements, thus elevating his mother's status.

His mother's death marked a critical moment in Confucius' life, both personally and professionally. Confucius was about twenty-four years old, his own children were very young and he was beginning his career as a civil servant and teacher. With her death, he no longer had a living parent and had two children of his own, making him the head of his own family and the sole person responsible for revering his family ancestors. He had spent much of his childhood and early adult years absorbing knowledge about history, traditional culture and rituals, and was now so well informed that he was in a position to form his own social philosophy and begin to teach it to others. His personal experience of mourning his mother's passing – one of the ultimate family rituals – equipped him to teach the value of human relationships, a concept that lay at the core of his philosophy.

4

Early Career and Teachings

Confucius' twenties were a time of major personal changes and challenges. He married, had three children and lost one, and his own mother died, leaving him without parents. This period also marked the beginning of his professional journey along the dual paths of his career – civil servant and teacher. Ever since his childhood he had studied the traditional rituals and the protocol surrounding the important ancestral sacrifices, as well as the songs and poems from the Zhou dynasty. Now, as an expert in the ways of the ancients, he hoped to find employment as a government adviser in ritual and protocol. Despite his family's aristocratic origins Confucius was merely a commoner, and at this point in Chinese history it was rare for a person of his low rank to attain an important government post. Such positions were generally assigned according to social status, rather than education or talent. However, his reputation as a diligent scholar and his determination to enter the civil service soon rewarded him with a low-level government job.

Around 530 BC, when Confucius was about twenty years old, he was appointed manager of the state's grain warehouse,[1] not a glamorous position but an important one, as grains such as rice and millet have long been the staple foods of China. This grain was often stored by governments to be used in case of famine; it was vital to protect it from insects and mould and keep precise records of the quantity available. Although his job kept him far from those who made major political decisions, Confucius worked diligently, keeping meticulous records of the state's holdings and making sure the grain was safe. He described his responsibilities in a very matter-of-fact manner. 'My calculations must all be right – That's all I have to care about'[2] he said, suggesting that he was contented with such a low-key post at this point in his career.

Within a year or two Confucius was promoted to a slightly higher government position, this time managing the state's herds of oxen and flocks of sheep. While working as husbandry manager he was equally conscientious, treating the job with importance and respect. Again he was very straightforward about his responsibilities, declaring, 'The oxen and sheep must be fat and strong and superior – that is all I have to care about.'[3] Such an attitude demonstrates focus and dedication to his work, as well as a humble, dignified acceptance of his social status. Two years into this appointment his mother died, and during the three-year mourning period he was required by tradition to refrain from working. So at this point he left the post and appears not to have returned to it.

These government jobs apparently did not pay enough to support his family, so at the age of about twenty-two, while still working as a civil servant, Confucius opened a school and began his career as a teacher. His school was probably within his home compound, either a room in his house or an area in the courtyard where he sat and delivered his lessons to a small class of students. As well as providing more income for his family, the school also gave him the intellectual stimulation and sense of importance that was missing in his government post. Though he did not complain about his official work he likely found it somewhat tedious, as it consisted largely of accounting and management, which were never his foremost interests. The opportunity to share with young, keen minds some of his knowledge of history, ritual and music undoubtedly sharpened his own intellect and motivated him at this formative stage in his career to begin to develop his own political philosophy.

In his early days as a teacher he did not focus on philosophical issues, as he had not yet evolved a social or political philosophy. Instead, he taught what he himself had spent years studying – history, rituals, music and poetry. He described his credentials as a teacher with the following words: 'He who by revising the old knows the new is fit to be a teacher,'[4] and he claimed that he was simply sharing his knowledge with others: 'I transmit, I invent nothing. I trust and love the past.'[5] He insisted that in order to understand the world and to better themselves, people should study the wise words of the ancients. In particular he advocated reading such texts as *The Book of Songs*, since these traditional songs or poems contained great moral wisdom, and he once claimed, 'The three hundred *Poems* are summed up in one single phrase: "Think no evil."'[6] However, he also strongly encouraged critical thinking and offered the following example of what could happen if study was not accompanied by careful thought: 'Consider a man who can recite three hundred *Poems*; you give him an official post, but he is not up to the task; you send him abroad on a diplomatic mission, but he is not capable of simple repartee. What is the use of all his vast learning?'[7] His overall approach to education is therefore best summarised by his statement, 'To study without thinking is futile. To think without studying is dangerous.'[8]

Confucius was somewhat selective about the students he allowed into his school and had two basic policies for admission. Firstly, they had to be intelligent and enthusiastic. According to *The Analects* he said, 'I only enlighten the enthusiastic; I only guide the fervent.

After I have lifted up one corner of a question, if the student cannot discover the other three, I do not repeat.'[9] Secondly, admission was open to students of any social class or background and was not restricted to the wealthy. Students paid what they could afford. He proudly claimed, 'From the very poorest upwards – beginning even with the man who could bring no better present than a bundle of dried flesh – none has ever come to me without receiving instruction.'[10] Clearly, though Confucius needed the income from his school to support his own family, it mattered more to him that his students be eager to learn than able to pay for tuition.

In his early twenties his knowledge of ancient history, ritual and music was already unrivalled in the state of Lu, and despite his relatively low social status he was regarded as a culturally sophisticated gentleman or *junzi*. As with the English word 'gentleman', the Chinese word 'junzi' originally referred to a male aristocrat who possessed various social and cultural skills, but by Confucius' day it could also be applied to a well educated commoner like Confucius. To Confucius, however, the concept of the gentleman was to take on a far deeper, more ethical meaning over the course of his life and career. In his teachings he described a true gentleman as a man of advanced learning and impeccable moral character, who was kind and considerate to others and behaved in a manner appropriate to his social status. Such a morally superior figure could then help raise the level of others he met, including the *xiaoren* who lacked moral virtue.[11] All his life he strove to live as a gentleman of exceptional moral calibre, and he occasionally lamented that he had not attained his goal. At one point he commented, 'A gentleman abides by three principles which I am unable to follow: his humanity knows no anxiety; his wisdom knows no hesitation; his courage knows no fear.'[12] As a young teacher, he certainly would not yet have considered himself a gentleman by his own standards but, fortunately for him, enough people in the state of Lu held his erudition in high regard, and his school was soon full of students.

His students came from all over, from the capital city to the countryside. Some were sons of aristocrats and were eager to study the history and rituals necessary to equip themselves properly for government office. Others, like Confucius, came from families who had once been part of the aristocracy but were now commoners. Perhaps some of them believed, as Confucius did, that the current unstable political situation and their own social status could only be remedied by learning from the past, and they looked to Confucius as a valuable source of ancient wisdom. Others still were sons of farmers, merchants, soldiers and craftsmen. These young men of modest means and backgrounds also sought his teachings, apparently hoping that by studying with him they too could become respected gentlemen with a sophisticated understanding of traditional culture. Many of the less wealthy students hoped to improve their lives by attaining government posts, as their teacher had done. All that his pupils had in common was that they were young men. Confucius had no female students, a fact that was not remarkable in his day, so was not commented on by his disciples or by early biographers or historians. Being considered socially inferior, women generally did not receive the same level and type of education as men.[13]

One of his first students was a teenager called Zilu (also known by his style name, or more formal name, of Zhong You), who came from a farming background but aspired to a career in politics. A rather brash fellow only nine years younger than Confucius, Zilu is said to have challenged him from their very first meeting. Confucius asked Zilu what he was most fond of. When Zilu replied that he loved his long sword, Confucius suggested that if he added an education to his swordsmanship, he would become a superior man. Zilu scoffed at this, saying that learning was of no use to him, as he was already able to take a strip of bamboo, cut it and sharpen it so that it could pierce a rhinoceros's hide. Confucius pointed out that an education would enable him to turn the bamboo into an arrow with a steel point and a feathered tail, and that such an arrow could pierce the rhinoceros's hide more deeply. At this Zilu bowed twice and said, 'I will reverently receive your instructions.'[14] Such an exchange, though perhaps only legendary, provides an insight into the characters of both young men: Zilu the rough, impetuous fighter, and Confucius the level-headed educator who could turn any conversation into an opportunity to learn. According to *The Analects*, Zilu remained impulsive and argumentative throughout his life, often receiving sharp criticism from Confucius for his fiery ways. However, even though they argued for decades, Zilu continued to be a devoted student of Confucius for many years. Confucius was deeply fond of Zilu, and years later he is said to have cried when he heard of Zilu's death in battle.[15]

As with his government position, his job as a teacher was also put on hold for three years (from age twenty-four to twenty-seven) while he mourned the passing of his mother. Although he had only been teaching for a couple of years by this time, he had apparently already formed close enough relationships with several of his students to delegate some of the funeral arrangements to them. After burying his mother and father together in a tomb and raising the burial mound over their coffins, he returned home and left a group of his students to oversee the completion of the structure. Visiting later that evening, it was the students that told Confucius of the tomb's collapse and witnessed their teacher burst into tears and lament that this was not the way tombs were built in antiquity.[16] Because he trusted his students with such an important task as the construction of his parents' tomb and then broke down emotionally in front of them, we can infer that even at the beginning of his career as a teacher he had a comfortable, familiar rapport with them. Such closeness was to be a feature of his relationship with his followers over the decades and undoubtedly contributed to their sense of mutual devotion.

After Confucius completed his period of mourning for his mother, he continued teaching at his school and advancing his own studies at the same time. It is not clear whether he was still employed by the state of Lu, but he seems to have had connections with the court that enabled him to pursue his interests in ritual and music. Perhaps because of his reputation as an expert in ritual, he was invited in 525 BC to attend a banquet hosted by Duke Zhao of Lu for the Viscount of Tan, a small state near Lu. The Viscount was a great orator, and at the banquet he lectured about the various rituals held in his state, including the sacrifices made to Shaohao, one of the earliest mythological Chinese emperors who supposedly reigned from c. 2597 BC to c. 2514 BC. Confucius was so captivated by the speaker and his vast knowledge that he stayed with him long after the banquet ended to find out all he could about the rituals of Tan.[17]

Confucius also studied music with Master Xiang, the chief bard of the court of Lu. Music was of great interest to him, in part because he derived immense pleasure from it, but also because he felt that it connected him with the people of ancient times. Under Master Xiang he learned to play music written by King Wen, one of the founders of the Zhou dynasty whom he greatly admired. He was deeply moved by these melodies and surmised that the music of the ancients 'in so far as one can find out about it began with a strict unison. Soon the musicians were given more liberty; but the tone remained harmonious, brilliant, consistent, right on till the close.'[18] From this statement it has been suggested that Confucius also considered music to be a metaphor for the development of the individual, as he strongly believed in the importance of understanding the rudiments of a subject before attempting to perform on one's own, or improvise.[19]

By his late twenties Confucius believed that he had mastered the basics of rites and protocol. He had spent his youth studying history and ritual and much of his twenties teaching the subject and perhaps even advising on etiquette at the court of Lu. His knowledge of both domestic protocol and that of the surrounding states meant that he could be invaluable at any diplomatic mission or treaty negotiation. He could ensure that the state's ceremonies and events were conducted correctly, without any risk of causing offence to local or foreign attendees. 'At thirty, I had planted my feet firm upon the ground.'[20] Confucius felt ready to be put to the test in an important official capacity.

It was around this time that Confucius caught the attention of a highly influential member of the government of Lu. In 518 BC, Meng Xizi, the chief minister of Lu and the head of the powerful Mengsun clan, was dying. On his deathbed he told his chief officer:

A knowledge of propriety is the stem of a man. Without it he has no means of standing firm. I have heard that there is one K'ung Ch'iu [Kongqiu, or Confucius], who is thoroughly versed in it. He is a descendant of sages, and though the line of his family was extinguished in Sung [Song], among his ancestors there were Fu-Fu Ho [Fu Fuhe], who resigned the state to his brother, and Ch'ang K'ao-fu [Zheng Kaofu], who was distinguished for his humility. Tsang Heh [Zang Sunhe] has observed that if sage men of intelligent virtue do not attain eminence, distinguished men are sure to appear among their posterity. His words are now to be verified, I think in K'ung Ch'iu [Kongqiu]. After my death, you must tell Hochi [his son Heji, or Meng Yizi] to go and study proprieties under him.[21]

Meng Xizi's words were taken very seriously by his successor, and they were to give a new direction to Confucius' career.

Soon after Meng Xizi's death his son and successor, Meng Yizi, and his brother (or close relative) Nangong Jingshu (also known as Nangong Guo), enrolled as students of Confucius. The wealth and prestige of these high-ranking students gave a considerable boost to Confucius' status as a teacher. In addition, as their tutor, Confucius received a stipend from the government and was encouraged to advance his own studies through research and travel. Almost immediately, Confucius decided to use his new status to arrange a trip to Luoyang, the capital of the Zhou dynasty. His new student Jingshu took his request to the Duke of Lu, who allowed him to go with Confucius and granted them a chariot, two horses and a page boy[22] for their journey. Other students may also have accompanied them to the capital, but Meng Yizi likely had to remain in Lu to carry out his duties as chief minister. Confucius' wife and children presumably remained at home and were supported by some of his stipend.

The journey to Luoyang was the first of many Confucius took out of the state of Lu. Unlike his later wanderings, however, this trip was entirely of his own volition, was fully funded, and was motivated by a desire for knowledge about his country and its history. The journey took him and his companions – who may also have included some other students – roughly 200 miles westwards across the northern Chinese countryside through the state of Wei (and possibly the state of Zheng) and into the state of Zhou, where the capital was located. It seems that, despite the ongoing rivalry between the various Zhou states, their trip was without political incident. Although they were sponsored by the Duke of Lu, this humble-looking group of scholars probably seemed unthreatening to local authorities and uninviting to bandits.

For much of the distance they probably followed and marvelled at the famous Yellow River, which winds 3,000 miles through northern China, from the Tibet–Qinghai Plateau to the Yellow Sea. The river derives its names from the millions of tons of yellowish-brown silt called loess that it picks up along its journey and then deposits as it approaches the sea, along a corridor known as the Yellow River Valley. The Yellow River is often referred to as the cradle of Chinese civilisation because the loess is highly fertile, and in Neolithic times agricultural communities rose up where the loess was deposited, planting such crops as millet, green onions and ginger. However, for centuries the river has been both a blessing and a curse for farmers, as the large quantities of loess often caused the river beds to rise and the water to pour over the walls and levees built by the farmers to protect their fields. The Yellow River has changed its course many times in history, delivering its blessings and curses to nearby inhabitants as it snaked its way through the region. Confucius is said to have once stood by a river and said, 'Everything flows like this without ceasing, day and night.'[23] Perhaps it was this powerful, relentless river that inspired his observation about the continuity of life.

After a week or two of travelling, the group arrived at the capital. The city of Luoyang, known in Confucius' time as Zhengzhou, was originally established in the eleventh century BC by the Western Zhou as a settlement for members of the defeated Shang court, but in 770 BC, under the weakened Eastern Zhou dynasty, the city became the capital of the Zhou Empire and was the centre of Zhou court and religious life. Although the Eastern Zhou kings had all but lost political power in their empire, they still maintained religious authority. They were in charge of the rituals dedicated to the powerful spirits of the Zhou ancestors and the sacrifices made to Heaven and Earth, and as such were responsible for maintaining harmony between the human world and the spirit world. As a city of ritual and ceremony, Luoyang held enormous appeal for Confucius, since it was here that the Duke of Zhou and other Zhou heroes were honoured. Until now Confucius had studied the history of the Zhou dynasty from afar. In their capital he was at the very heart of their world, the perfect place to expand his knowledge of Zhou history and ritual. Such knowledge, he hoped, would render him invaluable to the government of Lu on his return.

At Luoyang Confucius' primary interest was in the royal areas dedicated to ritual and ceremony. He visited the grounds where the Zhou rulers conducted sacrifices to Heaven and Earth and the temple dedicated to the Zhou ancestors. He avidly took notes on the arrangements of both sacred sites, perhaps with the intention of creating similar ones back in Lu. In the ancestral temple he noticed an unusual metal statue of a man with three clasps on his mouth and an inscription extolling the virtues of silence, and he encouraged his companions to heed this advice. He also visited the Zhou court and was particularly impressed by the Hall of Light, where the king received foreign guests. On the walls of the great Hall were paintings of ancient kings from the legendary Yao and Shun until the present Zhou ruler. Each painting bore the name of the ruler and an inscription containing words of warning and praise. This display was no doubt intended to impress any visitor to the Hall with the historical importance of the Zhou rulers. Confucius was profoundly moved by this and observed to his companions, 'Here you see how Zhou became so great. As we use a glass to examine the forms of things, so must we study antiquity to understand the present time.'[24]

Confucius was also keen to learn about music while in the royal city and met with a court musician by the name of Chang Hong. Typically, court musicians were blind, and Confucius pointed out this fact to his students on one occasion. But Chang Hong must have been an exception to this rule, as he was apparently impressed with Confucius' appearance, noting his 'river eyes' and 'dragon forehead', his long arms and great height. He was also struck by his knowledge of history and the ways of past kings, remarking, 'He moves along the path of humility and courtesy. He has heard of every subject and retains with a strong memory. His knowledge of things seems inexhaustible. Have we not in him the rising of a sage?'[25]

According to traditional accounts the high point of Confucius' visit to Luoyang was his meeting with Laozi, the philosopher who is often credited with founding Daoism and authoring its main text, the *Daode jing*. Laozi was an older man and worked as a librarian or archivist for the Zhou court. The two great men sat and talked about philosophy, and when Confucius was leaving Laozi offered the younger man some valuable advice: 'A shrewd observer, prone to criticise others, risks his own life. A learned man who exposes the faults of others endangers himself. A filial son must never thrust himself forward, and neither may a good subject.'[26] He also warned Confucius, 'I have heard that a good merchant, though he has rich treasures deeply stored, appears as if he were poor, and that a superior man whose virtue is complete, is yet to outward appearance seemingly stupid. Put away your proud air and many desires, your insinuating habit and wild will. These are of no advantage to you.'[27] Confucius left the meeting so amazed by the older man that he was briefly unable to speak. Then he recounted to his students, 'I know how the birds can fly, how fishes can swim, and how animals can run. But the runner may be snared, the swimmer may be hooked, and the flyer may be shot by the arrow. But there is the dragon. I cannot tell how he mounts on the wind through the clouds, and rises to Heaven. Today I have seen Lao-tsze [Laozi], and can only compare him to the dragon.'[28]

This meeting was supposedly a critical moment in Confucius' life, and the conversation between the founders of China's two principal philosophical systems has long been considered a highly symbolic moment in Chinese history, one which was depicted in art from as early as the Han dynasty. However, it is unlikely that Confucius and Laozi ever actually met. Early histories, including the work of Sima Qian, place Laozi in the sixth century BC as a contemporary of Confucius, but among modern historians there is great debate not only about when he lived, but whether he existed at all. Some scholars suggest that he lived during the fourth or third century BC, two or three hundred years after Confucius. Others argue that Laozi is a purely mythical figure or, more likely, a synthesis of various historical characters. A meeting with Laozi was therefore chronologically impossible. Confucius may indeed have met with an older philosopher in Luoyang and received some wise advice from him, but it is doubtful that we will ever know who this man really was.

Confucius probably spent several months in Luoyang, familiarising himself with the ways of the royal city. Back in Lu, he no doubt expected to be able to put his new knowledge to use in a government position, but shortly after his return the political situation there became so unstable that it was impossible for Confucius to remain in his home state. Lu was one of the weaker states in the Zhou territories at this point, and increasingly faced threats and harassment from some of the larger states and coalitions of states forming to the west and south. To preserve its independence, it may have in fact become a protectorate of its northern neighbor Qi, which was much richer but was also struggling to maintain its political power. Throughout most of his twenty-five-year reign, Duke Zhao of Lu had been plagued by internal strife, mostly caused by the power struggle among the Jisun, Mengsun and Shusun clans. The combination of internal and external conflicts had undermined his political, financial and military strength to such an extent that, around the year 516 BC, a relatively minor incident resulted in his downfall. A noble of the Jisun clan was involved in a cock fight with a rival nobleman and an argument broke out in which the Jisun noble insulted Duke Zhao. The Duke sent troops to arrest the offensive nobleman, who resisted. His clan then joined forces with the Mengsun and Shusun, and together the three rival clans forced the Duke to flee to Qi in the north. The Duke remained there in exile until his death several years later.[29]

Because of Confucius' close association with Duke Zhao, it was no longer safe for him to remain in Lu. Accompanied by several students, including Zilu, he followed the Duke to Qi, hoping his stay there would be brief. It is not clear whether his family went with him to Qi or remained in Lu, as texts typically do not mention his wife and children when recounting any of his travels. On the way to Qi he and his party passed by Mount Tai, China's most sacred mountain, according to Daoist beliefs. This legendary mountain sat on the border between the two states and was largely beyond the reach of the governments of either state. In this no man's land they encountered a woman who sat by a graveside weeping. Confucius sent his student Zilu to find out why she was crying. They learned that her husband's father and her husband had both been killed by a tiger at this spot, and her son had just met the same fate. Though saddened by her tragic story, Confucius asked her why she stayed in such a dangerous place. Her response was that this area was not ruled by an oppressive government. At this, Confucius, always the teacher, turned to his students and explained, 'My children, remember this. Oppressive government is fiercer than a tiger.'[30]

Upon his arrival in the state of Qi Confucius soon realised that he was in a civilised land. Even in the countryside the people seemed to be influenced by ancient culture. He caught sight of a young man carrying a pitcher of water who walked as if moving to the sound of ancient music, and urged his driver to hurry to the capital so that he could learn more about this state. Once there, he is said to have made the acquaintance of the chief court musician. With him Confucius discussed ancient music and studied the Coronation Hymn of the Emperor Shun, also known as *shao* music, and was so captivated by it that for three months he forgot the taste of meat. 'I never imagined that music could attain such perfection,' he exclaimed.[31]

Confucius soon gained an audience with Duke Jing, the ruler of Qi. The Duke of Qi was initially well disposed to Confucius, since he had apparently met him on an earlier visit to Lu. Confucius had given him valuable advice about how to make his own state more powerful, including the suggestions that a king should aspire to morally correct behaviour and that he should hire advisers on the basis of their merit and not their social status.[32] Now that Confucius was in Qi, Duke Jing questioned him more thoroughly about successful government practices and Confucius readily provided advice. The Duke was apparently so impressed by his conversations with Confucius that he offered him a small town to rule. But Confucius refused the gift, telling his followers that a gentleman should only receive a reward for services that he has performed, and since the Duke had not actually followed any of the advice he had given him so far, he could not accept his gift. 'Very far is he from understanding me!' he declared.[33]

Duke Jing continued, nonetheless, to question Confucius about government, and Confucius offered him some of his most profound words of political advice: 'Let the prince be a prince, the minister a minister, the father a father and the son a son.'[34] These words relate to his doctrine of 'Rectifying Names', which was supremely important in this theory of government. If a prince behaved in a tyrannical manner towards his people, Confucius argued, he should be called a tyrant, not a prince. If he stole from his people, he should be called a thief, and so on. To Confucius, the correct use of language was crucial to social order and peace. 'If the names are not correct, language is without an object. When language is without an object, no affair can be effected. When no affair can be effected, rites and music wither. When rites and music wither, punishments and penalties miss their target. When punishments and penalties miss their target, the people do not know where they stand.'[35] If all people at all levels of society behaved in accordance with their names, then a prince would be prince-like, ministers would be minister-like, a father would be father-like, and sons would be son-like. Over the course of history, some leaders have mistakenly interpreted this doctrine to mean that subjects should simply accept their positions in a strict social hierarchy and not question or challenge their leaders. In fact, Confucius had very strong views about what it was to be a true prince or minister. With their authority came great responsibility, he warned. Only if these leaders acted with benevolence and compassion towards their subjects would they deserve their respect, loyalty and obedience. The same principles applied to the smaller family unit, with each member acting with kindness and decorum according to their own position within the family.

It is possible that the Duke of Qi understood the true meaning of Confucius' advice. He went on to question Confucius further and was advised that he should also be very economical in the use of the state's wealth.[36] At this point the Duke was keen to retain Confucius in Qi and offered him another, larger, fief. Confucius might have accepted this generous position, especially if he felt that the Duke was beginning to heed his advice, but the Duke's chief minister, Yan Ying, and a number of other officials put up a strong resistance. Perhaps, as his chief minister, Yan Ying felt threatened by the Duke's interest in Confucius as an adviser. Years before, when Confucius had suggested to the Duke that he hire advisers on the basis of merit, Yan Ying may have taken this as an insult directed at him (which it may indeed have been) and held a grudge against Confucius ever since. Whether this was the case or not, it must have been infuriating for Yan Ying to be dealing dutifully with the various matters of the state while Confucius, a newcomer to Qi with relatively little political experience, spent hours with the Duke counselling him on how to improve his government. Perhaps it would have been more diplomatic of Confucius to include Yan Ying in such discussions, since Yan Ying was an intelligent man with significant experience governing the state. Then the two advisers could have shared their knowledge and experience and worked together to assist the Duke. Instead, Confucius seems to have had little interest in what the ministers from Qi had to say and was determined to guide Duke according to his own personal philosophy.

Other incidents demonstrated his lack of political sensitivity while in Qi. For example, in one case a minister arrived late for a meeting with the Duke and explained that he had been required to defend a man against persecution from a local dignitary. The Duke proudly told Confucius that this occurrence was proof of how virtuous his officials were, since the prosecutor had been willing to hear the defence. Instead of being impressed, Confucius bluntly told the

Duke that if his officials were so virtuous they would have hired reliable employees in the first place to avoid wasting so much time on such disputes. Confucius' response not only offended the minister who was late and insulted the prosecutor in the case, but it also belittled the Duke, who nevertheless apologised humbly to Confucius.[37]

This diplomatic weakness on Confucius' part could be attributed to his relative youth and inexperience in the political arena. However, his dealings with other officials appear to have remained more or less unchanged throughout his career. Later in his life, as he travelled from state to state seeking employment as an official adviser, Confucius seems to have continued to antagonise other local government officials in similar ways – not so much by actively offending them, but by choosing not to engage with them at all. His confidence in his own philosophy and his lack of interest in other officials was thus viewed as arrogance by the local ministers and, in state after state, ministers sought his removal from government office. This disregard for diplomacy may explain why he was not able to maintain a position as a government adviser for long enough to ensure that his teachings were adopted as policy by a ruler of his day.

Confucius had only been in Qi several months when, in an attempt to discredit Confucius and weaken his influence over Duke Jing, Yan Ying unleashed a tirade of what may be one of the earliest recorded criticisms of Confucius and his philosophy.

These Confucians are such unruly windbags, so arrogant and self-willed that there is no controlling them. They set great store by long mourning and bankrupt themselves for a sumptuous funeral; it would never do if this became the custom. A beggar who roams the land talking is not a man to entrust with affairs of the state. Ever since the passing of the great sages and the decline of the Zhou Dynasty, the rites and music have fallen into decay. Now Confucius lays such stress on appearance and costume, elaborate etiquette and codes of behaviour that it would take generations to learn his rules – one lifetime would not be enough. To adopt his way of reforming the state would not be putting the common people first.[38]

These hostile words from his chief minister seem to have convinced the Duke that Confucius was indeed merely an academic, a theoretician who was too attached to the past and had little experience of the present, real world. Worst of all, Yan Ying had pointed out some apparent contradictions in Confucius' political advice that made him appear inconsistent, or even insincere. Confucius had counselled the Duke to be economical in the use of wealth and to consider the good of the ordinary people, but he also advocated expensive, time-consuming funerals and other ceremonies that, if adopted by the population, could lead to financial disaster. The criticisms had their desired effect. Duke Jing began to distance himself from Confucius, withdrawing his offer of a fief and lowering Confucius' official status at the court of Qi, which restricted Confucius' access to the Duke. Eventually, the Duke claimed, 'I am old. I cannot make use of your services,' words that indicated quite clearly to Confucius that he was no longer welcome in Qi,[39] so he made preparations to leave.

Some accounts say that Yan Ying regretted his harsh words and visited Confucius one evening while he was entertaining in his quarters. He waited until all the guests had left and told Confucius that although he had been critical of his advice, he believed that the state of Qi really needed him, because it was heading towards danger, like the driver of a runaway chariot that was racing towards a cliff. He begged Confucius to remain in Qi. Confucius, however, was now committed to returning to Lu and told Yan Ying that it was already too late for the state. He predicted that the Duke himself would end his reign successfully, as would Yan Ying, but that their successors would be far weaker and would be overthrown by rival clans. There was nothing he could do to restore the runaway chariot to its correct course, even if he were to push it himself.[40]

Confucius and his followers soon left Qi and made their way back to Lu. Confucius was now approaching forty. His Duke was still in exile and he was returning to a politically unstable situation in Lu. He still hoped to serve in a government position there but did not have solid connections with the clans who currently held power, and still had little government experience. His first real attempt to serve as an adviser to a ruler had failed after only a few months, and he was forced to uproot himself again. Despite these setbacks, it appears that he had already developed some of his most important political theories regarding the responsibilities of a virtuous ruler, and he still had a loyal following of students who were eager to learn from him. Perhaps in part because of their devotion to his emerging philosophy, his self-confidence seems to have remained intact and his convictions stronger than ever as he headed towards his home state and towards political, professional and personal uncertainty.

5

Return to Lu

When Confucius and his followers returned to Lu sometime around 515 BC, they found their home state in political disarray. Duke Zhao of Lu remained in exile in Qi and those members of the Duke's family who had stayed in Lu lived there at the mercy of the Three Families, who had forced the Duke out. Although still officially merely advisers to the Duke of Lu, the Jisuns, Mengsuns and Shusuns had divided up the state and were now controlling it with the help of their large armies. Confucius regarded this new regime as illegitimate, since the three clans had deposed their own lord without proper justification. Confucius espoused the traditional belief that when rulers were corrupt, their subjects were not only entitled, but morally obliged, to rise up and overthrow them, as the Zhou had done with the Shang. This had not been the case in Lu; Duke Zhao was weak and ineffectual at worst, but he was not corrupt. When the Three Families chased him out, they had not acted in the interest of the Lu people but had merely seized power for themselves.

To Confucius, the actions of the Three Families signalled the beginning of the end of the state of Lu. He maintained that, in an ideal world, a king should rule virtuously over his realm, and below him princes and dukes should preside similarly over their states, advised in turn by wise ministers. Below them their subjects, the common people, should be peaceful and prosperous. Now, Lu not only lacked the strong rule of the Zhou kings, but it had also lost its own Duke and was run by its ministers. Lu's social structure had been undermined at the upper level, so peace and prosperity would be impossible to achieve. Confucius predicted that it was only a matter of time before the ministers were themselves overthrown by their own officers and Lu dissolved into total chaos.

Leading the three clans was the Jisun family, whom Confucius had long disdained, largely because of their lack of respect for propriety and their indifference to the correct performance of rituals. He had witnessed this attitude years before when, as a young man, he had managed the state's granaries and livestock, which were under the jurisdiction of the Jisun clan. Now that they had seized control from the Duke, the Jisun demonstrated an even greater disregard for propriety, so his contempt for them ran even deeper. *The Analects* provides several examples of Confucius' outrage at their irresponsible attitude to important ceremonies, all of which probably occurred after Confucius' return to Lu. On one occasion, the head of the Jisun clan decided to visit Mount Tai on a royal pilgrimage. Traditionally only the Son of Heaven was allowed to make sacrifices on this peak. When Confucius discovered that the Jisun leader intended to perform a highly sacred ritual meant only for the Zhou kings, he was incensed by this breach of religious protocol. He sought out his former student, Ran Qiu, who was at that time in the employ of the Jisun family, and implored him to prevent such a sacrilegious act. When Ran Qiu told him that he could do nothing to stop it Confucius was despondent and lamented loudly that he could not believe that the spirit of the mountain would allow such an indecent act.[1]

In another well known affront to the Zhou rulers and ancient ritual order, the Jisun clan organised a ceremony at their ancestral temple that employed the same number of participants as was reserved for the royal family. Traditionally, the king was allowed eight rows of eight dancers to perform the chanting, clapping and movements, a duke was permitted six rows of dancers, and ministers of feudal lords, such as the Jisun, were entitled to have four rows. The Jisun had eight rows of dancers, a clear signal to all in attendance that they considered themselves the equal of the king. Confucius was horrified by such a usurpation of royal privilege and declared, 'If he [the Jisun leader] is capable of that, what will he not be capable of?'[2] It seems that the Jisun and the other ruling families had no qualms about breaking any ritual traditions. According to *The Analects*, the Three Families also insisted on performing the poem *Yong* at the end of their ancestral ceremonies. This hymn was reserved for royal occasions, as is suggested in its lyrics: 'The feudal lords are in attendance. The Son of Heaven is sitting on his throne.' Again this irreverent conduct offended Confucius, and he questioned, 'What application can this have in the halls of the Three Families?'[3] Clearly, the families had no interest in propriety, and with each breach of tradition, Confucius believed, they were further upsetting the social order, which would have serious consequences.

A couple of years after Confucius returned to Lu, news came of the death of Duke Zhao in exile (*c.* 510) BC. This placed the Jisun family in an awkward position. The Three Families had not technically overthrown the Duke by assuming his title and destroying his family. They were still officially only the Duke's ministers, and as such they were now required to arrange for ceremonies to honour him, even though they had been responsible for his exile. They were also expected to appoint a successor, and tradition dictated that Duke Zhao's son should become the new Duke of Lu. But the clan once again flouted protocol and appointed the Duke's brother instead. The new Duke, generally known by his posthumous title Duke Ding, was now the lord of Lu, but the Three Families held on to their power and ensured that the Duke's position was only a nominal one. Initially, the presence of a new duke within the state made little change to its political power structure. Over time, however, as Confucius had predicted, the Three Families began to face challenges from among their own officers who sought to overthrow them, just as they had overthrown Duke Zhao.

The two officers who presented the greatest threat were Yang Hu and Gongshan Furao, both of whom held top positions as retainers for the Jisun family. These officers were well positioned in the government to observe its weaknesses and to rally others around them to mount significant rebellions against the Three Families. According to traditional accounts, both rebels attempted to involve Confucius in their plots and offered him government positions. At the time, Confucius did not hold an official post. Although he had long hoped to serve as a government adviser, he could not bear the prospect of working for a corrupt regime led by usurpers, and he believed that it was improper for a gentleman to align himself himself with such people. The idea of associating with the rebels, however, was also contrary to his beliefs, and Confucius appears to have been in a dilemma regarding the ethical issues that such an association might raise. The rebels planned to overthrow the usurpers and, as a loyalist to the usurped Duke, Confucius supported their cause. But the rebels had no intention of restoring the Duke to power and instead planned to rule the state themselves. As mere officers and ministers, they had no more place than did the Three Families at the top of Confucius' model of an ideal society, so he could not support them. It seems that Confucius was not willing to subscribe to the notion of the lesser of two evils.

At some point during the period of rebellion Confucius was

approached by Yang Hu, also known as Yang He or Yang Huo. He was the top-ranking minister of the Jisun clan and already held significant power in the state of Lu. He very likely assisted the Three Families in overthrowing Duke Zhao and, according to some accounts, he also acted against the Duke during his exile,[4] so it is not surprising that Confucius strongly disliked the man and considered him a traitor. In 505 BC Yang Hu turned against the Jisun clan. He held the current clan leader, Ji Huanzi, captive and forced him to accede to his terms before finally releasing him. Yang Hu is said to have invited Confucius to work for him. Although Confucius would no doubt have delighted in the downfall of the Jisun clan, he disliked Yang Hu for his treatment of the Duke and tried his utmost to ignore Yang Hu's offers of a government post. But Yang Hu was persistent. Taking advantage of the scholar's high regard for propriety, he sent a gift of a pig to Confucius' home when he knew that Confucius was away. According to protocol, when a minister sent a gift to a scholar and the latter was not home, the scholar was obliged to pay a courtesy call to the minister's home in return.

Confucius was now forced to visit Yang Hu, but he cunningly tried to outmanoeuvre Yang Hu by timing his visit so that Yang Hu would be away when he called. He arrived at Yang Hu's house and pretended to be disappointed when he was told the minister was out. On his way home, however, he bumped into Yang Hu, who had apparently suspected that Confucius might try this trick and was waiting for him. Yang Hu challenged Confucius in a manner that seems to have resonated with Confucius' sense of morality and purpose: 'Can a man be virtuous if he keeps his talents for himself while his country is going astray? I do not think so. Can a man be called wise if he is eager to act, yet misses every opportunity to do so? I do not think so. The days and months go by, time is not with us.' Despite his contempt for Yang Hu, Confucius had trouble disagreeing with his basic argument, and at the end of their conversation he reluctantly gave in and told Yang Hu that he would accept a government post.[5] There are no records of him actually working for Yang Hu, and it is possible that in this case he merely complied because he wanted the rebel to leave him alone.

The second officer seems to have been slightly more successful in piquing Confucius' interest. Gongshan Furao rebelled openly against the Three Families and captured the fortress town of Bi, which was the main stronghold of the Jisun clan. This was apparently his first move in an attempt to overthrow the Three Families and seize control of the entire state. Aware that Confucius' knowledge of history and ritual would be an asset to his government, the rebel invited the scholar to join him there and work in his new government. It seems that Confucius seriously considered this offer, since he had become increasingly eager to see the end of the Three Families' regime and to work in government again, but he met with resistance from Zilu. Confucius' loyal student was disappointed at his teacher's interest in joining forces with rebels, since this was not appropriate action for a gentleman. He beseeched his Master, 'It is too bad if we have nowhere to go, but is this a reason to join Gongshan?' Confucius replied, 'Since he invited me, it must be for some purpose. If only someone would employ me, I could establish a new Zhou dynasty in the East.'[6] Although Confucius ultimately chose not to join Gongshan Furao either, his desperation to be employed as a government adviser is apparent from this episode.

It seems that Yang Hu and Gongshan Furao were able to pose a threat to the Three Families for a number of years, but they were never actually successful in overthrowing the families, and eventually the rebels were forced eventually to flee from Lu and take refuge, as Duke Zhao and Confucius had done earlier, over the border in Qi.[7] The insurrections had taken their toll, however, on the Three Families, and once the rebels had left the state Duke Ding succeeded in gaining back some of his power and employed a new chief minister to replace Yang Hu. His choice was significant for Confucius, as the new minister was his faithful but feisty follower, Zilu. Within a year of Zilu's appointment, and no doubt with Zilu's recommendation, Confucius, at the age of around fifty years old, finally found himself being invited to join Duke Ding's government after more than a decade of waiting on the sidelines.

Very little was written in the early Chinese histories about Confucius during the fifteen or so years between his return to Lu and his employment by Duke Ding, namely where he was or what he was doing in his late thirties and forties. A few comments in *The Analects* do provide us, however, with some insight into his state of mind at the time. For example, he claimed, 'At forty, I had no doubts,'[8] suggesting that his confidence was unshaken by the various disappointing events of his thirties, including the exile of his lord, his failed attempt to serve as adviser to the Duke of Qi and his inability to find a government job in Lu. He also declared at some point that if, 'by the age of forty or fifty, a man has not made a name for himself, he no longer deserves to be taken seriously.'[9] It is possible that he made this statement earlier in his life, when he still imagined he would attain a civil service post. Perhaps the two statements together suggest that, at forty, he was more or less at peace with the idea that he was not going to become a government adviser, but had 'no doubts' about himself as a scholar and was content to devote himself to his academic research and teaching.

In another similar statement in *The Analects* regarding this age, Confucius said, 'Whoever, by the age of forty, is still disliked, will remain so until the end.'[10] It is tempting for this author to believe that the statement was a reference to his personal life. According to some accounts, Confucius divorced his wife around the year 510 BC, when he was forty-one and she was slightly younger.[11] That same year he married his daughter off to his follower Gongye Chang. His adult son Li, or Boyu, had become one of his regular students (he too married, but records do not indicate when). Perhaps the stresses and uncertainties of Confucius' career and the long stretches of time spent apart had strained their marital relations and made it impossible for them to live together after their children had grown up.

From contemporary records, we know that divorce was practised in the Zhou dynasty. In most cases it was the husband who divorced the wife, and there were ten grounds on which a man could do so, including adultery, barrenness, talkativeness and jealousy. A woman had fewer justifications to leave her husband, but she could divorce him if he beat her cruelly, deceived her in the marriage contract or deserted her, remaining away for three or more years without providing her with any support.[12] We know that Confucius travelled to Luoyang and Qi, and it is not clear how long he remained in either place, but he very likely left her alone to look after their family while he was away. He did not earn a significant income on either trip, so it is hard to imagine how his wife and children managed themselves in his absence. It is therefore possible that his wife sued for divorce on the grounds of desertion during these periods. It may be the case that Confucius himself instigated the separation in order to concentrate on his teachings at the school. The decision to separate could have been mutual – they simply found each other difficult to live with. Since they were both around the age of forty, they may have considered the situation unlikely to improve. Finally, although the question of his possible divorce is one of the most tantalising mysteries about

Confucius, as with many of the other pieces of his life puzzle, it may never have happened. As is implied by the ancestor tablet in the Confucius Temple in Qufu, on which both their names are inscribed as a couple, they may well have remained together, married, until his wife's death in 485 BC.

Other biographers have suggested instead that the statement about being disliked at the age of forty alluded to his professional situation. By this age, Confucius had probably resigned himself to a life as a political outsider as long as the Three Families remained in power. During the fifteen or so years after his return to Lu, there is no record of him being employed in government. This is hardly surprising given his critical attitude towards the Three Families and what he perceived to be their illegitimate usurpation of power. In his eyes, however, the fact that he had not been offered a position by the current regime was more a reflection of their moral deficiencies and poor judgement than of any deficiency in his own abilities. That the Three Families had not hired him was nothing for him to be ashamed of. In fact, it was more in keeping with the ways of a true gentleman to maintain a distance from a corrupt government, and it would be shameful for the gentleman to work for it. In *The Analects* he summarised his approach to dealing with such a regime with the following words: 'Uphold the faith, love learning, defend the good Way with your life. Enter not a country that is unstable; dwell not in a country that is in turmoil. Shine in a world that follows the Way; hide when the world loses the Way. In a country where the Way prevails, it is shameful to remain poor and obscure; in a country which has lost the Way, it is shameful to become rich and honoured.'[13] Apparently he had no interest in serving the Three Families to achieve glory or riches, since by doing so he would be showing himself to be a lesser man.

Instead of working for the government, it would seem that

Confucius chose to 'hide'. According to Sima Qian, because of the corrupt nature of the Lu regime under the Three Families, 'Confucius took no official post but edited *The Book of Songs, Book of History, Book of Rites* and *Book of Music* in retirement'.[14] Over the centuries it has been the tendency of historians and biographers to accept Sima Qian's claim that Confucius spent these years editing, compiling and writing commentaries on the texts that later became the core canon of Confucianism. *The Book of Songs, The Book of History* and *The Book of Rites*, along with *The Book of Changes* and *The Spring and Autumn Annals*, make up the Five Confucian Classics which have long been required reading for all students of his philosophy.[15] We know that these works already existed in some form in his lifetime, because he himself studied some of the texts as a young man; and in *The Analects* he refers on a couple of occasions to *The Book of History*, and we read that he encouraged his son, Boyu, and his other students to read *The Book of Songs* and *The Book of Rites* as a means of sharpening their minds and cultivating their characters. While it is certainly possible that during these years Confucius devoted his time and energy to working on those texts, his exact role in the creation of what became the standard version of these important Confucian classics cannot be confirmed.

Sima Qian also notes that during this period, 'more and more pupils came even from distant places to study under him'.[16] Again, his professional situation at the time is uncertain but, because of the many different students mentioned in *The Analects* and other texts, it does seem likely that the number of his followers grew considerably. Having begun his school in his early twenties, Confucius was now a highly respected teacher with some government experience and a broader outlook on the world than many people of his day, so it is probable that many students from far afield sought to be educated by him. As before, his curriculum focused mainly on history, ritual, literature and song, and discussions of politics were no doubt common. Even though he is known to have said, 'He who holds no official position discusses no official policies,'[17] it is not difficult to imagine Confucius, an ardent critic of the Three Families, instructing his students about correct government practices using the golden age of the early Zhou period as the model of an ideal regime and the current administration as an example of government gone awry, of the world 'losing the Way'.

During this period some of his older students, including Zilu, remained with him, his own son, Boyu, also becoming a follower. Many new students also added great colour and vivacity to his classroom (see Chapter 6). The diversity of backgrounds, generations and geographical regions represented by the students who gathered at his academy undoubtedly helped to make the decade or so that he spent 'in hiding' as a teacher a stimulating time for Confucius. Although he had longed to work in the government, the opportunity to spend so many years researching the classics and the ways of the ancients and discussing and debating them with such a lively group of bright, enthusiastic minds would have contributed greatly to the sense of satisfaction that he seems to have experienced in his forties. As he witnessed the Three Families act with disregard to tradition, it seems likely that his belief in the necessity of propriety and ritual only strengthened. As he watched these usurpers and the various rebel leaders tear apart the basic structure of Lu society, his convictions about the importance of this hierarchy were sharpened. As he observed his students commit themselves to study and develop many of the virtues required of a gentleman, he realised more than ever how essential education and moral cultivation were for people who wished to right social wrongs. At forty, Confucius apparently had no doubts in his mind about what it would take to set his kingdom on an even keel again. A decade later his confidence reached an even higher level. In *The Analects*, he is said to have stated, 'At fifty, I knew the will of Heaven.'[18]

It was when Confucius reached fifty that his student Zilu, as chief minister to Duke Ding, recommended that Confucius be assigned a government position. In 501 BC Confucius was appointed Chief Magistrate of Zhongdu, a town in Lu near the northern border with Qi. This was Confucius' first government position in Lu since he had worked as a state husbandry manager in his early twenties. It seems that he was given this assignment far from the capital to test his abilities as a governor. If he succeeded he could be brought closer to the centre of power, but if he failed his post was in such a remote area that any damage he might cause would not impact on the rest of the state. Confucius was pleased to accept the job now that Duke Ding was at the helm, with the Three Families largely relegated to the role of his advisers again. After many years of theorising about how society should be run and criticising those who did it badly, Confucius was eager to put his theories into practice. He once declared, 'If a ruler could employ me, in one year I would make things work, and in three years the results would show.'[19] Now he finally had a chance to prove himself.

Confucius appears to have been true to his word. As the ruler of Zhongdu, he began by establishing himself as a moral example for his people, confident that, like a moral polestar, he could inspire his people to strive for higher standards.[20] He went on to enforce the correct observation of rituals and protocols, both for the living and the deceased. According to certain texts, he assigned rules to govern the nourishment of the living and observances to the dead. Different foods were fed to the young and the old, and different burdens were given to the strong and the weak. Burials were stream-lined and simplified, with coffins made to specific dimensions and thicknesses and graves built on high ground, without being cov-ered with mounds or surrounded by trees. He ensured that the people of the town behaved according to their social position and with consideration towards each other. The older and stronger showed kindness to the younger and weaker, and were rewarded in return with obedience and respect. Males and females now respectfully kept apart on the street, and if an object was dropped on the road, passers-by would leave it so that its owner could return to reclaim it.[21] Of this period in Confucius' career Sima Qian notes simply that 'after one year of administration, all the neighbouring districts were following his example.'[22]

Duke Ding was impressed by Confucius' achievements in Zhongdu and asked him if he thought his rules for government could be applied to a whole state. When Confucius replied that they could even be applied to an entire kingdom, the Duke imme-diately promoted him to Assistant-Superintendent of Public Works, one of the three main branches of the Lu administration, the others being Civil Affairs and Military Affairs. In this position, although he reported directly to the head of the Mengsun clan, who was a chief adviser to the Duke, Confucius was no doubt pleased now to be at the centre of Lu government and close to the Duke. In the Public Works department he apparently surveyed the lands of Lu and made some improvements to agriculture. He was also given the politically delicate task of dealing with the placement of the tomb of Duke Zhao in the royal cemetery. After his body had been returned to Lu, the head of the Jisun clan, still bitter towards the Duke even after his death, had ordered that his grave be situated at a distance from the other royal tombs. Confucius was aware that this would isolate the Duke from his family in his afterlife, but he could not go against the will of the Jisun family. So, as a compromise, he arranged for a ditch to be dug around the entire cemetery, thus uniting the tomb of the Duke and those of his family in a single, delineated area. When the Jisun leader questioned him about this act, he claimed that he had done it to hide his own disloyalty towards the Duke.[23] This response seems to have appeased, and perhaps even impressed, the Jisun leader, who pushed the issue no further.

Shortly afterwards, in either 500 or 499 BC, Confucius was promoted to the position of Minister of Justice of the state of Lu, the highest position he was ever to attain in government. It was probably in his capacity as chief law-maker of the country that he was invited by Duke Ding to go with him to the village of Jiagu on an important diplomatic mission, which had the goal of preventing further conflict with the northern state of Qi.[24] The two states had been antagonistic neighbours for over a century. They intermittently took up arms against each other, and on many occasions enemies of the Lu government, such as Duke Zhao and his followers (including Confucius several years before) and later Yang Hu and Gongshan Furao, were granted asylum within Qi's borders. Now, it appeared that Duke Jing of Qi was prepared to enter into a peace treaty with Duke Ding of Lu, so that the two states could end their conflict and focus their resources on defending themselves from other aggressors. Duke Ding realised that Confucius, with his extensive knowledge, would be an invaluable assistant at such a critical meeting, and Confucius was honoured to accompany the Duke. From the outset, Confucius apparently did not trust the Duke of Qi's motives and recommended that Duke Ding also bring along military officers, saying, 'I have heard that in peace men should prepare for war; in war they should prepare for peace. In the old days a baron never left his territory unless accompanied by military officials.'[25]

It turned out that Confucius was right to be suspicious. Apparently the Duke of Qi and his ministers were plotting to kidnap Duke Ding, and they planned to cause a distraction while Duke Jing's own troops then seized Duke Ding. At the meeting the two dukes sat upon a platform and prepared to negotiate the terms of their peace treaty. Soon Confucius, who was serving as Master of Ceremonies for the Duke of Lu, noticed a group of men armed with pennants, feathers, spears, swords and the like approaching accompanied by the sound of drums. He protested, 'Our two rulers are meeting in friendship: what is the meaning of this barbarian music? Let these men be dismissed by the officer in charge!'²⁶ He may have been reacting out of concern for his lord's safety, but it is more likely that he thought the music highly improper for such a serious occasion as the signing of a peace treaty. To Confucius, propriety concerning music and ceremony was of extreme importance, and the group from Qi had breached protocol. The Duke of Qi was embarrassed and ordered his chief officer to send the men away. Then another group of jesters, singers and dwarfs trooped up to the platform offering to perform palace music. Again Confucius was outraged and exclaimed, 'Commoners who beguile their lords deserve to die.' Apparently the performers were then put to death.²⁷ The Duke of Qi's officer in charge, who had been supervising these musical distractions, was Yan Ying, Confucius' old adversary at the court of Qi. Yan Ying had undoubtedly been dismayed to see Confucius arrive at the meeting with the Duke. Now that Confucius had foiled their plans to kidnap Duke Ding he was furious, but he had no choice but to obey his lord.

After this failed attempt to disrupt the meeting and abduct Duke Ding, Duke Jing of Qi was forced to begin the peace summit in earnest, and the negotiations began. He demanded that the Duke of Lu send him 300 chariots of war that he could use in Qi against his foes. In return Duke Ding, apparently advised by Confucius, demanded that Duke Jing return to Lu some areas of land that Qi had seized from the state of Lu in the past. The Duke of Qi conceded this as a way of apologising for the earlier ritual insult caused by the musicians and performers. The two parties agreed to the terms and signed a peace treaty. At the conclusion of the ceremony the Duke of Qi proposed some entertainment, but Confucius again spoke out, declaring that after such a solemn agreement a rowdy celebration would be inappropriate, particularly in such a wild region so far from Luoyang. They left hastily and returned to the Lu capital. Confucius' final statement was based in part on his concern for protocol, but he was also acting out of precaution, since he suspected that Duke Jing might still have been planning to overwhelm the Duke of Lu, using the entertainment as a distraction. Whether or not this was indeed his plan, the Duke of Qi and his entourage appear to have left the meeting in disgrace at having been outwitted by Duke Ding's Master of Ceremonies.[28]

This meeting was probably the high point of Confucius' political career. He had not only been able to help Duke Ding to negotiate a peace treaty with a hostile neighbouring state, but he had probably saved his life. He had used his intelligence and his knowledge to prevent a bloody battle between the two states. Furthermore, he had been able cleverly to turn a potentially dangerous situation to the advantage of his lord by shaming his enemy into agreeing to return territory that they had previously taken from Lu, thus expanding the Lu kingdom. That Lu had promised Qi 300 chariots seemed minor in comparison with the return of its precious lands. For Confucius this diplomatic mission must have been deeply satisfying, since it allowed him to fulfil his professional goal of serving as a wise adviser to a seemingly decent lord. He returned to the capital with the respect and gratitude of Duke Ding and with the reputation of being a shrewd politician who possessed remarkable powers of judgement.

After Confucius' return to the capital, his judgement was tested on many occasions as Minister of Justice. One of the most famous cases that he is believed to have overseen was that of a father who sued his own son. A highly unusual legal situation in any culture at any point in history, this dispute represented for Confucius a painful breakdown at the very heart of the social order, namely the relationship between parent and child. It is not clear exactly what the father was accusing the son of, but Confucius' ruling demonstrated considerable balance. He is thought to have consulted with various advisers, including some of his own students, and in the end he had both father and son locked up in jail for three months. He then dismissed them both. The leader of the Jisun clan was apparently baffled by Confucius' decision, saying, 'You are playing with me, Sir minister [sic] of Crime. Formerly you told me that in a State or a family filial duty was the first thing to be insisted on. What hinders you now from putting to death this unfilial son as an example to all the people?' To this Confucius replied, 'When superiors fail in their duty, and yet go to put their inferiors to death, it is not right. This father has not taught his son to be filial; – to listen to his charge would be to slay the guiltless. The manners of the age have long been in a sad condition; we cannot expect the people not to be transgressing the laws.'[29]

From this statement we learn that Confucius was determined as Minister of Justice to put into practice his belief in reciprocity – the idea that the responsibilities of any relationship fall on both individuals. Certainly the son, as the junior of the pair, should have shown respect and obedience towards his father, the senior, but he was unable to do so because his father had not educated him adequately in the rules of proper behaviour and had perhaps himself not provided an example of such behaviour for his son. Here Confucius could not blame the son entirely because if he had been better brought up he would not have caused his father such distress. Fault lay, therefore, with both parties. Confucius then took this argument one step further by suggesting that the ultimate blame for this sad familial dispute lay with the government of Lu, which had not set a good example to its people in recent years. Because of the political turmoil of the last decade or so, with ministers overthrowing dukes and officials attempting to overthrow ministers, how were ordinary people expected to know how to behave? Confucius repeatedly stressed to his students that virtue was a quality that needed to begin at the top of society and filter downwards. The transformation could take time, he warned. Even with a benevolent leader, it could be an entire generation before morality was restored to the country, but eventually, with good leaders in charge for one hundred years, cruelty and murder would cease.[30] Only under such virtuous rulers would the people know how to behave.

With this basic principle in mind, Confucius is believed to have used his position as Minister of Justice to attempt to reform the government of Lu so that it could function in a manner that he regarded as beneficial to the state. Although Duke Ding was officially the ruler of Lu, the Three Families still held tremendous power, and often defied his will and threatened revolt when they opposed a particular policy he was promoting. A source of much of their influence lay in the fortified towns that each clan possessed. These walled cities, defended by impressive armies, enabled the clans to put up armed resistance against the Duke at almost a moment's notice. Confucius suggested to the Duke that, as the ruler of Lu, only he should possess a defensible site. 'A subject should not conceal arms,' he advised, and 'a noble should not have city walls over three thousand feet long'.[31] With the help of two of his

fellow advisers, Zilu and Ran Qiu, both of whom were his followers, Confucius was able to convince Duke Ding that he should
dismantle these other fortified cities in order to prevent the clans
from opposing him and to stop rebels from seizing the towns and
mounting a rebellion against the central government, as Gongshan
Furao had done at the Jisun stronghold of Bi. The Duke agreed
with the plan, and somehow managed to convince the Shusun family
to disarm its stronghold in the city of Hou. The Jisun clan, however, put up a strong resistance. Gongshan Furao still controlled
Bi and not only refused to dismantle the city but also sent Jisun
troops to the capital to fight the Duke. They apparently forced the
Duke and some of his ministers to retreat into a tower, while his
army battled the Jisun soldiers. Eventually, perhaps with Confucius in command of some of the men, the Duke's forces overcame
the Jisun and the city of Bi was demolished, and Gongshan Furao
fled to Qi.[32] The third clan, the Mengsun, was determined not to
give up its stronghold, the town of Cheng. Its leader remained
within its walls, resisting the Duke's forces in a stand-off that wore
on for several months, until the Duke finally retreated and left the
Mengsun in control.

Even without capturing the Mengsun's stronghold, it seems that
Confucius and his fellow advisers were able to restore to the Duke
much of the power that had been wrested from him and his predecessor by the Three Families. For this the Duke was no doubt
extremely grateful to Confucius, and would have rewarded him
accordingly. Sima Qian records that in the fourteenth year of Duke
Ding's reign, when Confucius was in his mid-fifties, the Duke
appointed him Prime Minister. He apparently appeared highly grati-
fied, which surprised his students, who remarked 'We have heard
that a gentleman would show no fear in the face of calamity, no
joy in the face of good fortune.' To this Confucius replied, 'True,

but what of the saying, "He delights in high position because he can show his humility"?'[33] Although Confucius was probably not actually promoted to such a high position in government,[34] the episode nonetheless suggests that Confucius was pleased at this point in his career to be able to advise his Duke so closely. According to Sima Qian and other questionable accounts, Confucius used his influence to transform the state of Lu. In a short period of time merchants supposedly stopped raising the prices of goods, people became more honest, men and women behaved more honourably towards each other and strangers were welcomed.[35]

Some of these strangers may have returned to their states with stories about the positive transformation of Lu society under Confucius' influence. Apparently, to the north of Lu in Qi, the ruling house and its ministers, who were still smarting from their humiliation by Confucius at Jiagu, began to worry that if Lu continued to prosper under Confucius' administration it might become strong enough to swallow up its neighbours, no doubt beginning with Qi. Certain ministers recommended currying favour with Lu by surrendering more territory to the Duke, but this idea was overshadowed by a proposal to try to drive Duke Ding and Confucius apart. With this aim in mind, the government of Qi sent the Duke a 'gift' of eighty beautiful dancing girls and sixty pairs of dappled horses. The dancers and horses were brought outside the capital and Ji Huanzi, the head of the Jisun family, went out in disguise to inspect them. He was captivated by the women and persuaded the Duke to accept the gift. For three days Ji Huanzi and the Duke neglected the state's affairs in order to spend time with the dancing girls. Confucius was deeply disappointed in their immoral conduct, as was his follower and colleague Zilu, who suggested to him that it was time to leave the Duke's government.

Confucius was unwilling to abandon his lord and determined

to wait a little longer, until the conclusion of an important ceremony at which the Duke was to conduct sacrifices to Heaven and
Earth. 'If he presents portions of the offerings to the ministers, I
can stay,' he vowed. Unfortunately, when the time came to make
the sacrifices, the Duke rushed through the rituals and neglected
to reward his ministers with portions of meat from the sacrificial
animal, which was the established custom. He then carried on his
irresponsible behaviour, paying no attention to Confucius and his
other advisers. At this point Confucius had to concede that his
Duke was not the virtuous ruler he had hoped for, and prepared
himself to resign his post and retire from office. The head of the
Jisun clan apparently sent a note questioning his resignation but
gave no indication that he or the Duke intended to change their
ways. Rather than serve a lord whose morals were shameful, he
chose to leave his position as one of the most powerful men in
Lu.[36] So disappointed was he in his Duke that he walked away not
only from the government, but from the state of Lu as well. Confucius' walk was to continue for fourteen years, as he and a handful
of his most devoted followers, including Zilu, wandered from state
to state in their quest for a ruler virtuous enough to serve.

6

Confucius' Followers

Around 496 BC Confucius left Lu for the third time in his life. His first trip to Luoyang in his twenties had been an exciting adventure to the capital that had lasted several months and inspired him enormously in his research. His second departure was in his mid-thirties, when he had followed his lord, Duke Zhao, to Qi and remained there in exile for about a year. Now, at age fifty-four, when most men in government positions were contemplating their imminent retirement, Confucius resigned from his job, gathered a few belongings and again crossed the border of Lu, this time in search of more satisfactory work. As he departed, he cannot have anticipated that his journey would keep him away from Lu for fourteen years. In those years he made his way to the neighbouring states of Wei, Song, Cai and Chen and was employed for short periods by rulers of some of those states, but otherwise he and his group were travelling around the region, at a time when relations between the states were highly volatile. He surely did not imagine that he would have to venture far and frequently in search of work or that he would not be able to find anywhere a virtuous ruler to serve. Nor did he guess that there would be times when he would experience homelessness and even starvation.

A number of Confucius' followers chose to go with him, which meant giving up their jobs, leaving their families and binding themselves tightly to Confucius' fortunes. Such personal and professional sacrifice was a testimony to how deeply they believed in his doctrines and how fondly they regarded their Master. During the three decades he had been teaching, hundreds, perhaps even thousands, of students passed through the gates of his school. Sima Qian wrote that Confucius himself claimed, 'Of those who received my teachings, there are seventy-seven who are conversant with them.'[1] Some of these are named in *The Analects*, and occasionally this text gives us insight not only into their characters, but also what Confucius supposedly thought of them. For example, he once drafted a list in which he grouped his main pupils according to their various gifts and abilities – great virtue, great eloquence, the ability to govern, and culture.[2] More information about his followers was provided by Sima Qian, who wrote brief biographies of thirty-five of the most famous of them, and noted the names of the remaining forty-two who were supposedly also conversant with their Master's teachings. These early (though, alas, not contemporary) descriptions provide insights into some of the colourful characters who studied with Confucius and help us to understand why some were devoted enough to their Master to leave everything behind to follow him on his long journey abroad.

Zilu

It is almost certain that Zilu (542–480 BC) was one of the students who accompanied Confucius on this fourteen-year journey, as there are several references in *The Analects* and other texts to incidents along the way involving him. (It is possible that Zilu had also been Confucius' companion on his two earlier travels to Luoyang and to the state of Qi.) As we have already seen, Zilu was one of the first young men to study with him when Confucius began teaching in his early twenties, and he is considered by many to be one of the most fascinating of Confucius' followers. Raised in the countryside in Lu, Zilu was a headstrong character who tended to act impulsively. Confucius thought highly of Zilu's acumen and believed he would be effective in government, but he also considered him wild and on several occasions tried to encourage him to slow down and think before he acted, commenting, 'If to your present ability were added the results of learning, you would be a very superior man.'[3] He criticised Zilu for passing judgement 'on the mere basis of half the evidence,'[4] and predicted correctly that the combination of his rash behaviour and lack of discernment would lead him to an unnatural and violent death.[5] Confucius made it clear to Zilu that he felt that his other student, the mild-mannered Yan Hui (see below), was closer to him in temperament and the type of man he would wish to have by his side in a crisis. When Zilu asked him whom he would have as his lieutenant, Confucius told him, 'I would not choose a man who wrestles with tigers or swims across rivers without fearing death,' clearly implying Zilu.[6] Confucius also declared, 'Yu's [Zilu's] delight in prowess surpasses mine. He is no material I can use.'[7]

Judging by the number of times Zilu is mentioned in *The Analects* questioning Confucius about how best to govern and become a gentleman, he was clearly a devoted student who was trying in his own way to cultivate his character and be a better man. He was a very keen student and 'loved to accompany [Confucius] on his travels.'[8] Yet Confucius was often highly critical of him. For example, when Zilu asked him about death and how to serve the spirits and gods, Confucius answered sharply, 'You are not yet able to serve men, how could you serve the spirits? ... You do not yet know life, how could you know death?'⁹ Much later, when Confucius was very ill and seemed on the verge of dying, Zilu organised his followers into a retinue as if they were retainers of a lord, in order to give him a funeral suited to a high-level government minister. When Confucius recovered, he was furious with Zilu for creating such a 'farce' and 'sham.'¹⁰ Such constant criticism and disapproval seems to have led Zilu to crave the approval and praise of his Master, as can be witnessed in two rather touching episodes. Confucius once told his students, 'The Way does not prevail. I shall take a raft and put out to sea. I am sure Zilu will accompany me.' Zilu was overjoyed at this idea, but Confucius was apparently merely joking about building a raft and suggesting that only Zilu would be foolhardy enough to try such a thing.¹¹ At another time, Confucius actually praised Zilu, saying, 'Only Zilu can stand in his tattered gown by the side of people wearing fine furs without feeling any embarrassment,' and went on to quote a verse from *The Book of Songs*: 'Without envy and without greed, He must be a good man.' Zilu was so delighted at the praise from his Master that he apparently chanted this verse continually, until Confucius burst his bubble with the remark, 'Come on, this is not the recipe for perfection.'¹²

Although Zilu seems to have received more criticism than praise from Confucius over their years together, he was of a strong enough will to deal out similar censure when he believed his Master was not following his own teachings or behaving as a gentleman should. We have already learned that he urged Confucius not to join the rebel Gonghsan Furao's government, even though Confucius seemed to think that the role might enable him to create a better government in Lu. In a similar incident, Confucius was invited by Bi Xi, the steward of a great family in the state of Jin, to the north-west of Lu. Bi Xi was using his position as governor of Zhongmou to mount a rebellion against his own lord, and Confucius was tempted to go to speak with him. Zilu was again outraged and threw Confucius' own words back at him. 'Master, in the past I heard you say "A gentleman does not associate with those who are personally committing evil ..." How can you contemplate joining him?' Confucius conceded that those were indeed his words, while at the same time lamenting the fact that he was not being put to use. Again, he listened to Zilu.[13] In both instances Zilu appears to have been trying to protect Confucius from temptation and from behaviour that was unfitting for a gentleman. Zilu was not always successful. On another occasion on their long journey, while Confucius and his group were staying in Wei and hoping to find employment with Duke Ling, Confucius received an invitation from the Duke's wife Nanzi, to visit her. Although Nanzi was a woman of questionable reputation, Confucius believed that protocol required him to accept her invitation and he did so. After the visit, which was conducted in an appropriate manner, Zilu was furious that Confucius had associated himself with such a woman and again chided his master, but this time after the fact.

Despite their complex relationship over the years and their differences of opinion and behaviour, Confucius and Zilu, separated by only nine years of age, remained close and grew to be old men together. Of all of his followers Zilu was arguably his most devoted, and this dedication was clear on many occasions. As Confucius had predicted, Zilu was indeed successful in attaining a job in the Lu government despite his rural background. Zilu undoubtedly felt that he owed his post to his Master, and so, shortly after his own appointment, he used his own authority to make sure Confucius was hired by Duke Ding. Later, acting out of the same sense of gratitude and loyalty to his mentor, Zilu joined Confucius in resigning his hard-earned position and followed him as a loyal retainer on his journey out of Lu. (After Confucius eventually returned to Lu, Zilu remained in the state of Wei serving the Duke. He died in his early sixties in a battle, loyally fighting to defend his lord who had treated him so well.)

Zigong

Another student who is also believed to have joined Confucius on his great journey was Duanmu Si, best known by his courtesy name, Zigong (b. 520 BC). According to Sima Qian, Zigong was a native of Wei, to the west of Lu,[14] and he must have travelled a considerable distance to study under Confucius. He joined Confucius' school during the period when Confucius was focusing on teaching and research in his thirties and forties, so is one of the second generation of students who were roughly thirty years younger than their Master. Zigong appears to have been one of Confucius' brighter, more enthusiastic and accomplished students and is mentioned often in *The Analects*, usually questioning Confucius on how best to become a true gentleman. Confucius generally thought well of him and once gave him high praise in a discussion about what it takes to be a *junzi*. Zigong asked Confucius if the following would be a good description of a good man: '"Poor without servility; rich without arrogance." How is that?' Confucius replied, 'Not bad, but better still: "Poor, yet cheerful; rich yet considerate"' To this, Zigong quoted *The Book of Songs*: '"Like carving horn, like sculpting ivory, like cutting jade, like polishing stone." Is this not the same idea?' Confucius was delighted that Zigong could allude so skilfully to the important text in a discussion about refining one's character. He exclaimed, 'Ah, one can really begin to discuss the *Poems* [*Songs*] with you! I tell you

Portrait of Confucius, Chinese
rubbing from a stone stele
engraved with an image based on
a painting by Wu Daozi (680–740)
© *akg-images*

Confucius' birth heralded by the
appearance of the mythical unicorn-like
animal, the Qilin, Chinese painting
© *Mary Evans Picture Library*

Cave in Ni Mountains, Shandong Province where Confucius was born
© *Werner Forman Archive / Scala, Florence*

Das Kind Khung Tsee mit seinen Gespielen.

Confucius as a child acting out religious
ceremonies as play, German engraving
© *Mary Evans Picture Library*

Confucius teaching his students, Chinese
painting
© *Mary Evans Picture Library*

Portrait of Yan Hui, Confucius'
favourite student, Chinese painting
© *The Granger Collection / TopFoto*

(*left*) Portrait of Zilu, Confucius' most loyal student, Japanese woodblock print by Tsukioka Yoshitoshi (1839–92)
© *Asian Art & Archaeology, Inc./CORBIS*

(*middle*) Confucius conferring with dukes of the Chinese states, Chinese painting
© *The Granger Collection / TopFoto*

(*bottom*) Confucius and followers wandering and studying, Chinese painting
© *Mary Evans/AISA Media*

Confucius and followers, early 20th-century Chinese
woodblock print with hand colouring
© *Pacific Asia Museum*

Confucius' Tomb, Qufu, Shandong
Province, China
© *Werner Forman Archive*

論語學而第一　何晏集解

子曰學而時習之不亦說乎有朋自
遠方來不亦樂乎人不知而不慍不
亦君子乎有子曰其為人也孝弟而
好犯上者鮮矣不好犯上而好作亂
者未之有也君子務本本立而道生
孝弟也者其仁之本與子曰巧言令

The first page of *The Analects of Confucius*,
Japanese 19th-century woodblock printed
book
© *Pacific Asia Museum*

A Confucian classroom (*Sodang*), Korean colour print
by Kim Hong-Do (1745–1806)
© *National Museum, Seoul, Korea / The Bridgeman Art Library*

Exams for military officers (*left*) and for men of letters (*right*), Vietnamese
19th-century colour litho print
© *Ecole Francaise d'Extreme Orient, Paris, France / Archives Charmet / The Bridgeman Art Library*

Main Hall of the Confucius Temple, Qufu, Shandong Province, China
© *Tibor Bognar / Alamy*

Red Prayer Plaques at the Confucius Temple, Qufu, Shandong Province, China
© *Courtesy of author*

Statue of Confucius in the Confucius Temple, Hanoi, Vietnam
© *AA World Travel Library / TopFoto*

Portrait of Confucius, 19th-century Korean painting
© *akg-images*

Portrait of Confucius, Japanese painting by Kano Tan'yu (1602–74)
© *The Granger Collection / TopFoto*

Portrait of Confucius, an engraving on ink on
paper from *Confucius Sinarum Philosophus*,
Paris, 1687

© Photo Scala Florence/Heritage Images

Statue of Confucius on Campus of California
State University at Los Angeles

© Courtesy of author

one thing, and you can figure out the rest.'[15] Confucius clearly relished such conversations with bright young minds like Zigong, as he considered them to be quicker-witted, more emotionally generous and less rigid than men of his own age. Sparring with them apparently kept his own mind sharp and helped him to formulate his thoughts more clearly.[16]

Although Confucius admired Zigong for his quick and clear mind, he did not apparently rank him among those of his students who possessed great virtue. Zigong did not seem to mind this assessment and himself once conceded to Confucius that he could not compare with Confucius' favourite student Yan Hui in virtue or intelligence. Confucius' response to this admission was revealing: 'Indeed, you are not his equal; and neither am I.'[17] On another occasion, when Zigong asked Confucius what he thought of him, Confucius replied, 'You are a pot.' This was not a flattering response from the Master, who had taught that a gentleman should not be like a container or vessel, with a finite capacity and a specific function. Unperturbed, Zigong then asked, 'What sort of pot?' to which Confucius replied, 'A precious ritual vessel,' showing Zigong that although he had not yet acquired the qualities of a gentleman, he was still of great value.[18] Perhaps Confucius had reservations about Zigong because the latter was also very interested in commerce, and Confucius was not. According to both Confucius and Sima Qian, Zigong was talented in business and became extremely wealthy.[19] The historian also describes Zigong as a shrewd political figure who was later appointed Prime Minister of Lu and of his native state of Wei. At one point in his career, Zigong served as a foreign minister of sorts and succeeded in saving Lu from an attack by Qi by skilfully manipulating other neighbouring states so that they chose to fight each other and spare Lu.[20]

Zai Yu

Zai Yu (520–481 BC) is another student who may have accompanied Confucius on at least part of his longest journey. Also known by the courtesy name of Ziwo, Zai Yu most likely joined Confucius' classroom during his teaching and research period. He appears to have shared Zigong's gift of quick and clear speech.[21] Zai Yu seems to have been argumentative and stubborn, which no doubt made for lively and stimulating discussions, so he was of great use to Confucius as a teacher who enjoyed honing his own skills on his students. On one occasion he cleverly challenged Confucius with the following conundrum: 'If a truly humane man, a *renren*, is told that someone is stuck in a well, would he go down the well himself to see what he could do [not worrying about his own safety]?' Confucius replied, 'Why would he do that? A gentleman, a *junzi*, can go and take a look but he is not going to hurl himself into a trap. He can be deceived but not ensnared.'[22] Here, Zai Yu is trying to force his teacher to admit that a gentleman, if truly compassionate (*renren* literally means 'compassionate man'), would attempt to help someone suffering without thinking of his own safety. Careful not to be caught in an intellectual trap himself, Confucius replies that the gentleman is not only very caring but also very careful, so would not recklessly risk his own life to save another.

Although Confucius enjoyed such intellectual challenges, he did not consider clever speech to be as valuable as thoughtful actions and he appears to have been repeatedly exasperated by Zai Yu's behaviour. Once, he found Zai Yu sleeping during the daytime, which was not acceptable for his students. He declared, 'Rotten wood cannot be carved; dung walls cannot be trowelled. What is the use of scolding him?' He added, 'There was a time when I used to listen to what people said and trusted that they would act accordingly, but now I listen to what they say and watch what they do. It is Zai Yu who made me change.'[23] In one of the tensest exchanges recorded between the Master and any of his students, Zai Yu questioned Confucius about the need to spend three years mourning a deceased parent, noting that such a long time away from one's other responsibilities, including rituals and music, would result in their decline. He suggested that one year would be quite long enough to mourn, as that amount of time corresponded to nature's seasons. Confucius asked Zai Yu, 'If after only one year, you were again to eat white rice and to wear silk, would you feel at ease?', to which Zai Yu replied, 'Absolutely'. Confucius was shocked by Zai Yu's lack of concern for his parents and respect for the traditional mourning rituals and chided, 'In that case, go ahead! The reason a gentleman prolongs his mourning is simply that, since fine food seems tasteless to him, and music offers him no enjoyment, and the comfort of his house makes him uneasy, he prefers to do without all these pleasures. But now, if you can enjoy them, go ahead!' Clearly, Confucius was implying here that his student did not possess the qualities of a gentleman. Once Zai Yu had left the room, he went even further and proclaimed to those still in the room with him, 'Zai Yu is devoid of humanity!'[24]

Ran Qiu

Even more infuriating to Confucius than Zai Yu was Ran Qiu (b. 522 BC). Also known by the name Ziyu, or Ziyou, Ran Qiu probably joined Confucius during the same period as Zai Yu. When he was a student, Confucius had ranked him along with Zilu as someone who would make an able government minister.

As predicted, Ran Qiu soon attained a government post under the Jisun clan, but he apparently failed to put into practice Confucius' lessons about benevolence and compassion, so Confucius later revised his opinion of him. On one occasion the head of the Jisun family was about to attack an autonomous region and claim it for himself. Confucius was outraged and asked Ran Qiu why this was happening. His former student replied, 'It is our master's wish, it is not the wish of either of us.' Confucius reprimanded Ran Qiu: 'Qiu! Is it not you who should be blamed for this? ... What sort of assistant is he, who cannot steady his master when he totters, nor support him when he trips?'[25] (It will be remembered that Ran Qiu was equally ineffectual in dissuading the head of the Jisun clan from making an irreverent pilgrimage to Mount Tai.)

On another occasion, when one of Confucius' wealthier disciples, Gongxi Chi, was sent on a mission to Qi, Ran Qiu granted Gongxi Chi's mother a huge allowance of rice while her son was away. Confucius apparently frowned upon this misplaced generosity, saying, 'I have always heard that a gentleman helps the needy; he does not make the rich richer still.'[26] Eventually Ran Qiu's seemingly blind loyalty to the Jisun family and his lack of sympathy towards the poor was too much for Confucius. When he found out that Ran Qiu was pressuring the peasants to pay higher taxes and further enrich the Jisun family, Confucius said, 'He is my disciple no more. Beat the drum, little ones, and attack him; you have my permission.'[27] Although Confucius was presumably speaking metaphorically here, such violent language is unusual for him and must be an indication of his deep dismay at his student's lack of compassion towards the less fortunate, and his frustration that he had not been able to teach him successfully. Nonetheless, despite Ran Qiu's inability to follow Confucius' teachings and his Master's despair at his lack of integrity, Ran Qiu is believed to have been one of the students who joined him on his travels. It is possible that he still hoped to learn something from Confucius and become a better man, though some scholars have suggested that he was simply going along for the ride and wanted to find a good job wherever his Master was finally employed.[28]

Yan Hui

Of all of his followers, Confucius' great favourite was a young man called Yan Hui (521–481 BC). Yan Hui, also known as Ziyuan, probably became his student when Confucius was already in his late forties, just before he was hired in the Lu administration. Yan Hui may have been a distant relative of Confucius, perhaps a cousin on his mother's side. Yan Hui came from a humble background and spent most of his life in poverty. Confucius praised him for his lack of interest in material wealth: 'Worthy indeed is Hui! A bamboo bowl of food and a gourd cup of drink in a shabby alley: other men could not bear such sorrow, but Hui does not vary in his joys.'[29] An apparently very contented young man, Yan Hui never challenged Confucius in his teachings, which sometimes frustrated Confucius and led others to believe that he was somewhat simple-minded. However, Confucius pointed out, 'Hui seems foolish. When I observe his private conduct after he has taken his leave, it is sufficient to illustrate [my teachings]. Hui is no fool.'[30] In fact, to Confucius he was the one of all his students who possessed the moral character closest to that of a gentleman. 'Ah!' he once declared, 'Yan Hui could attach his mind to goodness for three months without interruption, whereas the others manage this only now and then.'[31] As we have noted above, Confucius actually considered Yan Hui morally superior to himself and remarked at one point to Zilu that neither of them could match Yan Hui in virtue. Furthermore, Confucius is said to have believed that his students were closer to him when Yan Hui was around, either because they liked the young man so much or because Yan Hui brought out the best qualities in their Master.

Despite Confucius' high praise for his moral accomplishments, the humble Yan Hui apparently lacked confidence in his own intellect and questioned his progress as a student. At one point in *The Analects*, when Confucius was explaining to him how to practise benevolence by taming the self and observing rituals, Yan Hui replied, 'I may not be clever, but with your permission, I shall endeavour to do as you have said.'[32] Another passage in *The Analects* offers a touching glimpse of Yan Hui's impassioned struggle truly to grasp his Master's teachings. 'Yan Hui said with a sigh, "The more I contemplate it, the higher it is; the deeper I dig into it, the more it resists; I saw it in front of me, and then suddenly it was behind me. Step by step, our Master really knows how to entrap people. He stimulates me with literature, he restrains me with ritual. Even if I wanted to stop, I could not. Just as all my resources are exhausted, the goal is towering right above me; I long to embrace it, but cannot find the way."'[33] Yan Hui's confession helps us to understand why he was Confucius' favourite student. Like his teacher, his wish to educate himself and cultivate his character stemmed from more than a hope of attaining government employment or social status as a gentleman. It grew from a deep spiritual need to find 'the Way' and perfect himself, and it was this need that pushed him on, even when he was close to despair. As with Confucius, the desire to be a true gentleman seems to have been the very force that animated him. Confucius certainly recognised this and described him on occasions as the only student of his who truly loved learning. Sadly for Confucius, Yan Hui died young (at around forty), and Confucius lamented, 'Alas, I watched his progress, but I did not see him reach the goal.'[34] His death caused Confucius great despair.

Ran Yong

Another notable student who may have joined Confucius' group of travellers was Ran Yong (b. 522 BC). Ran Yong, also known by his courtesy name, Zhonggong, was from a humble family of farmers, but Confucius saw in him considerable virtue and paid him higher praise than any of his students other than Yan Hui. Confucius described Ran Yong as 'good but not eloquent', but to him this was hardly a problem, since one as honourable as Ran Yong would have no need for a clever tongue.[35] Confucius believed that his integrity was in fact so great that the young man had the makings of one who could be 'given the seat facing south',[36] meaning that he thought Ran Yong could become more than a government minister. He could rise to the position of the ruler of a state. When challenged about his student's humble origins, Confucius countered, 'If the calf of a plough ox has a sorrel coat and well-formed horns, would the [spirits of the] mountains and rivers refuse to accept it even though people may not want to use it [as sacrifice]?'[37] This is a fine example of Confucius' somewhat revolutionary belief that a position should be granted on the basis of a person's talent, merit and virtue rather than their birth. His students from lower social backgrounds, including Ran Yong, undoubtedly found great inspiration in this concept and their devotion to their Master grew because of it.

Min Ziqian and Ran Boniu

Along with Zilu, two other students had joined Confucius in his early days of teaching and remained loyal to him for many years, possibly even accompanying him on part of his journey. While Confucius believed that Zilu was destined to work in government, he considered Min Ziqian and Ran Boniu, along with Yan Hui and Ran Yong, as students who possessed great virtue.[38] Min Ziqian (b. 536 BC), also known as Min Xun and Ziqian, was a few years younger than Zilu and was supposedly a deeply filial son, endearing him greatly to Confucius. We have little information about his life, but he apparently demonstrated his high moral standards when he was offered the position of knight to one of the grand masters of the state, but 'refused to take the wages of a corrupt lord'.[39] Ran Boniu (born *c.* 544 BC), also known as Ran Gong and Boniu, was only a few years younger than his teacher and was also a man of immense integrity. Little is known about his life either, but when he was seriously ill, perhaps with a contagious disease such as leprosy, Confucius is said to have held his hand through the window and lamented, 'It is fate, isn't it! Such a man, yet with such a disease!'[40]

Boyu

It is possible that his own son Boyu was among his entourage as he travelled from state to state. Boyu is known to have joined his father's school in his twenties, and from what we can tell from *The Analects* and other sources, where he is only mentioned on a couple of occasions, he does not seem to have been a particularly gifted student or one with whom Confucius had memorable exchanges. Since, at the time of Confucius' departure, Boyu was a full-time student with his father and had not yet taken up employment, it is probable that he was still financially dependent on Confucius. If he did indeed join his group of followers, it may not have been simply out of devotion to his father and teacher. He probably did so partly for financial reasons.

With Yan Hui, Zilu, Zigong and a handful of other devoted students at his side, Confucius was blessed with both companionship and intellectual stimulation on his long and arduous travels from state to state. Although he had spent many hours in the classroom with them, it was probably in the years that they travelled together that the most important teaching and learning took place between Confucius and his followers. They confronted many challenging situations on the way, each challenge presenting an opportunity to examine their own characters, test their moral fortitude and put the teachings of their Master into practice. The journey also undoubtedly brought the group closer together on a personal level, as they spent many years in each other's company. It is easy to imagine tensions rising between some of the students and a certain amount of competition for their Master's praise, but it seems that they remained fond of their Master throughout their time abroad. Their devotion no doubt provided Confucius with the moral and physical support that he needed to undertake the journey. Whenever he failed to find work under a particular ruler or resigned in disappointment from the court of another, they were there to back his decision and encourage him to find another place to take his talents. On the occasions when Confucius was lost or in physical danger, one or more of his followers was there to rescue him. Finally, at those rare moments when Confucius appeared to be straying from his own moral path or giving up on his own beliefs, his students, in particular Zilu, were there to remind him of the strength and importance of his own teachings. Without the company and encouragement of his loyal students, it seems unlikely that Confucius would have been able to survive such a long, arduous ordeal and return to his home state of Lu.

7

The Wandering Years

There is very little reliable information about the journey that Confucius and his followers took between the years 496 and 484. We cannot be sure exactly where they were, at what time and for how long they stayed, but what we do know is that when Confucius and his followers crossed Lu's westernmost border and entered the kingdom of Wei, they left behind them the relative safety of their home state and embarked on a rather risky ordeal through politically volatile territory. Once they left Lu and Duke Ding, Confucius and his followers were not only unemployed and homeless, but they were stateless and, more importantly, lordless – a vulnerable position that placed them at the mercy of the lords and political fortunes of each kingdom they visited.

During the early part of the Eastern Zhou dynasty (770–475 BC), which is known as the Spring and Autumn period, the area that now makes up China comprised over one hundred separate states, all of which were theoretically under the rule of the Eastern Zhou kings, who – confined to their capital of Luoyang and a small royal domain surrounding it – in reality had no political strength. The states around them were largely autonomous, and during much of Confucius' lifetime they vied with each other for territory and power. Borders shifted constantly as the larger, more belligerent states

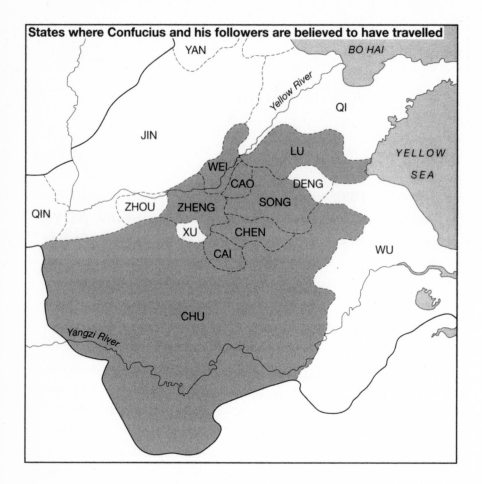

States where Confucius and his followers are believed to have travelled

invaded their smaller neighbours, annexed their territory and absorbed their resources. At this time, five in particular grew in strength – Qi, Song, Jin, Qin and Chu. Alliances were formed as lesser neighbouring states joined forces with each other to protect themselves from the larger aggressors, but the same alliances were often broken as soon as the larger states offered the smaller ones protection in return for help in defeating one another. Rulers observed each other closely, aware that an attack could come from any direction at any time, and they often chose to attack first rather than be attacked. Within their own states they valued military skill and loyalty from their people, and in return they offered them the protection of the state army. Without such a lord an individual had no protection, no matter how well respected he might be as a gentleman scholar.

The state of Wei

Once they left the capital of Lu, Confucius and his group set out with a chariot and some supplies and travelled 120 or so miles west to Wei. Here they planned to stay with Zilu's brother-in-law, who they hoped could help them find employment there. When they reached the boundary of Wei, the local warden in charge of the border asked to meet Confucius and his followers. The warden apparently sympathised with their predicament and told Confucius not to worry that he had been unable to maintain his position in Lu. 'The world has been long without the principles of truth and right; Heaven is going to use your master as a bell with its wooden tongue.'[1] Such friendly and encouraging words at the outset of their journey suggested that Confucius' wisdom was respected abroad and that the group might be well received in Wei.[2] Indeed,

Confucius had long considered the two states to be politically akin, remarking once that 'In politics, the states of Lu and Wei are brothers.'[3] He had followed Wei's politics very closely and was familiar with its various counsellors, commenting at one point that even though the ruler, Duke Ling, was himself lacking in principles, his state was still strong. Confucius credited Duke Ling's staff of fine counsellors for this strength: 'He has Kong Yu in charge of foreign affairs, Priest Tuo in charge of the ancestors cult, and Wangsun Jia in charge of defense. Under such conditions, how can he lose his state?'[4] Even though he was unsure of the moral calibre of the Duke of Wei the fact that he surrounded himself with such wise men gave Confucius hope that he too might find such a position in his government.

The group arrived in the capital of Wei and stayed initially at the home of Zilu's brother-in-law, who may have held a position in the government. Later the group stayed with Qu Boyu, a man forty or so years Confucius' senior whom Confucius greatly respected as a thinker and gentleman. The Duke of Wei soon heard of their arrival and inquired how much Confucius had been paid by the state of Lu. When he was told that he had received 60,000 measures of rice the Duke matched the sum, and for a while Confucius and his followers lived off this income. It is not clear whether the payment was for Confucius' services as an adviser to the Duke or merely a stipend to Confucius in acknowledgement of his reputation as a scholar. After ten months or so, however, Confucius decided to leave Wei and head for the state of Chu. The reason for his departure is unclear, but judging from earlier incidents in his life, if he had not actually been employed by the Duke, he may have become tired of waiting to be put to work (despite the generous salary). It is also possible that he was actually employed in Duke Ling's court and that quite early on in his tenure he had already started to make enemies among the other government officials. Indeed, Sima Qian recorded that someone slandered Confucius to Duke Ling and the Duke had a guard sent to watch over him, either out of concern for Confucius' safety or possibly out of distrust of him. Whatever the reason, he noted that Confucius sensed trouble brewing and prepared to leave Wei.[5]

According to traditional accounts, Confucius and his group decided to travel south to the state of Chen and so made their way there through the state of Zheng. While in Zheng they passed by the city of Kuang, which had suffered badly under the rebel Yang Hu a few years earlier when he had swept through the region. Unfortunately Confucius bore a slight resemblance to Yang Hu, and when his driver pointed to the city wall and remarked to Confucius that he had once entered the city through a gap in it, some local men were alarmed and mistook Confucius for Yang Hu returning to cause further destruction. They immediately arrested Confucius and detained him. His students were apparently not seized, and after several days his favourite student, Yan Hui, was able to convince his captors to release him. Greatly relieved, he exclaimed to Yan Hui, 'I thought you were dead.' Yan Hui's response was one of utter devotion: 'How dare I die when you are still living, Master?'[6] His other students, though also relieved that their Master was released, were deeply distressed by the aggression of the people of Kuang towards him. Confucius attempted to reassure them all with a declaration of his Heavenly mission. 'Since King Wen is no more, who but I can be the standard bearer of culture? If Heaven had wanted culture to disappear, I should not have possessed it after all this time. And if Heaven does not intend culture to disappear, what can the men of Kuang do to me?'[7] Despite this confidence, however, Confucius changed his plans to go to Chen, and the group made their way back to Wei.

Once back in Wei, Confucius received his invitation from the notorious wife of the Duke to pay her a visit.[8] The Duke himself was a man of questionable moral character, but his wife, Nanzi, was even more notorious for her sexual intrigues and immoral behaviour. She was from the neighbouring state of Song and before her marriage to Duke Ling she had been having an incestuous relationship with her brother. Apparently, the Duke generously invited her brother to join them in Wei, to the great shock and titillation of his people. Confucius was no doubt aware of her reputation, but since she was the wife of the Duke and had invited him to visit her in a very socially proper manner, it was difficult for him to refuse the invitation without offending her. It has been suggested that he may also have hoped that by meeting her he could curry her favour and increase his chances of finding a position in the government.[9] He reluctantly went to see her at the palace. According to Sima Qian, the encounter was conducted with suitable decorum. 'The lady sat behind a linen curtain to receive him. Confucius entered, facing north, and bowed low. She returned his bow behind the curtain and her jade pendants tinkled.'[10] When Zilu found out he was furious and reminded Confucius that a gentleman like him should not associate with a woman who had such a terrible reputation. Confucius apparently believed that propriety had required him to accept her invitation and exclaimed somewhat dramatically, 'If I have done wrong, may Heaven confound me! May Heaven confound me!'[11]

It seems that even after Zilu's remonstrations Confucius was obliged to have further contact with Nanzi, and this ultimately made it impossible for him to remain in Wei. Shortly after his first visit to her, Duke Ling invited him to join him and his wife in some sort of procession that may actually have been held in Confucius' honour. Apparently, the Duke and his wife rode in the first carriage, with

Confucius and Nanzi's eunuch escort in the carriage behind them. The people of Wei saw the incongruity of this display and shouted out, 'Lust in the front; virtue behind!' Confucius was ashamed, and made the very cynical observation, 'I have not seen one who loves virtue as he loves beauty.'[12] After this incident Confucius supposedly gave up hope of finding satisfactory employment under the Duke, gathered his followers and left Wei in disgust.

It was perhaps at this point in their exile, when it appeared as if Confucius and his followers might never be put to good use in government, that he asked them to share with him their dreams and aspirations. 'Forget for a moment that I am your elder,' he insisted. 'You often say: "The world does not recognise our merits." But given the opportunity, what would you wish to do?' Here Confucius apparently wanted to hear from them how they thought they might apply their learning and what they hoped to achieve if they were given adequate support. Zilu was the first to reply, saying that he would like to be given a country to run that was not too small but was squeezed between powerful neighbours, under attack and in the grip of famine. He vowed that within three years he would revive the spirits of the people and set them back on their feet. Ran Qiu then stated that he would like to control a domain of sixty or so leagues in size. Within three years he would secure the prosperity of the people but, as for their spiritual well-being, they would have to await the intervention of a true gentleman. A third student, Gongxi Chi, said that he wished to be given the opportunity to learn and that, during an event such as a diplomatic conference at the Ancestral Temple, he would like to wear a chasuble and cap and participate in the ceremonies as a junior assistant.

A fourth student, Zeng Dian, who was playing the zither when asked, admitted that he was nowhere near as ambitious as his three colleagues, saying he would simply like to take some time early in the year, after the spring clothes had all been made, and go with several companions to bathe in the River Yi, enjoy the evening breeze and sing. Here Confucius astounded his followers by sighing and saying, 'I am with Dian!'[13] His suggestion that he would rather go swimming in the river than try to solve a country's problems appeared to contradict his teachings and his serious character. Perhaps, having tried for so long to find a stable, satisfying government job, Confucius was now experiencing a moment of resignation to his fate. A gentle swim in a river suddenly seemed more pleasant than struggling against the turbulent waters of the current political scene. It has also been suggested that Confucius was exhibiting a different, rather mystical aspect of his character, more interested in relaxation and contemplation than in the rigorous tasks and responsibilities of political life.[14] However, he may simply have been displaying a light-hearted and playful attitude in the hope that a touch of whimsy might help lift his students from their despair.

The states of Cao and Zheng

There is some disagreement about where Confucius and his followers went after they left Wei, but traditional texts say that they began to travel southwards, heading again for Chen. They first travelled through the tiny state of Cao, which lay between Wei and Song, and were approaching the border of the larger Song, when Confucius experienced what was probably the most hostile reception of his entire life. The group had stopped just before the border and Confucius was giving his students a lesson about ritual under a large tree. Suddenly, from out of nowhere, a group headed by the Minister of Military Affairs of Song, a man by the name of Huan Tui, cut down the tree under which Confucius was standing in an attempt to kill him. The tree narrowly missed him. The Master seemed relatively unperturbed by the attack and responded by declaring, 'Heaven has implanted virtue in me. What can men like Huan Tui do to me?'[15] His followers, on the other hand, were distressed and urged him to hurry away from the spot.

There is much that is mysterious about this incident. We do not know, for instance, why Huan Tui wanted to kill Confucius. It has been suggested that he was an ally of the rebel Yang Hu, who supposedly had not forgotten Confucius' refusal to serve with him and wanted Confucius killed, but there is no evidence of their connection.[16] It has also been proposed that Huan Tui had been discredited by one of Confucius' students who was employed by the Song court, and when he found out that Confucius was nearby had decided to take out his anger on the Master himself.[17] Whatever the motivation may have been, if indeed Huan Tui wanted to harm Confucius it seems curious that he chose such an ineffective method of assassination, rather than simply slaying him with an arrow or sword. The tree missed its target, both physically and psychologically. Confucius not only survived but faced the danger of the moment with the same confidence and bravado that he demonstrated when he was captured in Kuang. Convinced that the importance and virtue of his teachings gave him Heavenly protection, Confucius was completely free from fear. Instead of fleeing in terror, he responded to the attack by trying to allay the fears of his students.

After this violent incident near Song the group realised that they might not be welcome there and so travelled west to Zheng, where Confucius was previously detained. Along the way, Confucius somehow became separated from his group and when he arrived in the capital he stood alone by the Eastern Gate of the city waiting to be received or at least to rejoin them. His followers were apparently already there, and a local man remarked to Zigong that he had seen a man standing by the East Gate who had 'a forehead like Yao, a neck like Kao Yao [Gao Yao] and shoulders like Tzu-chan [Zichan], and just three inches shorter below the waist than Yu. Lost as a stray dog he looks!' Zigong went to find his teacher and repeated what he had been told about his appearance. Confucius chuckled when he heard the description and replied, 'The appearance is unimportant, but it is true that I am like a stray dog. That is certainly true!'[18]

The state of Chen

After leaving Zheng the group made their way southwards to Chen, where they planned to settle for some time. They spent at last a year in Chen – perhaps, as Sima Qian claims, as long as three years.[19] It seems that they arrived at a very unstable time in Chen's history. While they were there, the state was attacked by at least three of its neighbours. The powerful state of Wu to the south-east invaded Chen at one point and took control of three of its towns. Directly to the south, the great state of Chu invaded Chen's western neighbor, Cai, and formed an alliance with that tiny state. Chu then proceeded to invade Chen at least once. The leaders of Chen, no doubt feeling increasingly threatened by their neighbours, appear to have consulted with Confucius on several occasions.

One day, a falcon was found dead at the court of Chen. It had been shot by a very long and unusual thorn arrow with a head made of stone. Duke Min of Chen decided to consult Confucius to find out who had shot the arrow. Although Confucius never regarded himself as an expert in weaponry and warfare, his knowledge of history was unsurpassed and he was able to draw on this expertise and to solve the mystery of the arrow. He immediately recognised it as a Sushen weapon.[20] The Sushen were a nomadic tribe of non-Chinese people who lived beyond the northern borders of the state of Yan in the north-eastern region of China. Apparently when King Wu of the Zhou dynasty had conquered the Shang in the eleventh century BC, he had demanded of various tribes outside his domain that they send him tribute. The Sushen had sent him some thorn arrows just like this one, eighteen inches long with a stone head. Later, when his daughter had married Duke Hu of Yu, he had presented her husband with Chen as well as the Sushen arrows as her dowry. Since Confucius knew that Duke Hu was the ancestor of the current Dukes of Chen, he deduced that the arrows were probably part of the Chen state's armoury. He told the Duke as much. When Duke Min checked his armoury, he discovered similar arrows there, thus proving that the falcon had been shot by one of his own nobles.[21] It has even been suggested that the Duke may have shot the falcon himself and brought the arrow to Confucius to test his knowledge.[22] Whether or not this was the case, the Duke is said to have been very impressed by Confucius' remarkable grasp of history and his ability to apply it to solving present-day problems.

On the move between states

Although he was admired and valued in Chen for his exceptional knowledge, Confucius and his followers were distressed by the number of attacks being made on the state by its neighbours, so they decided to leave and take to the road again. According to Sima Qian, Confucius was keen at this point to return to Lu and declared to his students, 'Let us return! We may be ambitious, reckless fellows, but in our quest we do not forget our origin.'[23] Unfortunately for the teacher and his loyal entourage, the journey back to Lu was to take several more years, as they encountered various obstacles along their dangerous route northwards through politically volatile territory. For example, when they were passing through the city of Pu (probably located within Wei territory) a rebellion broke out, and the party was caught up in the conflict and detained by the rebels. One of Confucius' disciples was a tall, strong fellow called Gongliang Ru, also called Zizheng, who had been with Confucius when they were captured at Kuang. Apparently he was determined to help Confucius break free of their captors, or at least die trying, and he put up such a great fight that the captors became afraid of the group. They agreed to let them go on the condition that they did not return to Wei. Confucius gave his word and they were allowed to leave the city. Despite his promise, however, Confucius proceeded to travel towards Wei. When Zigong questioned him about breaking his word, Confucius simply reasoned, 'I gave it under pressure: the gods will not count it.'[24] To Confucius, his tireless belief in his Heavenly mission not only propelled him onwards in his journey across the country; in a time of lawlessness and unrest, it also provided the justification for breaking a few promises made to rebels along the way.

Return to Wei

When they arrived back in Wei for the third time, Duke Ling was apparently delighted to hear that the Master had returned and asked Confucius for advice about invading Pu, where Confucius and his colleagues had just been held by the rebels. Rather than pursue a peaceful policy, Confucius surprisingly encouraged Duke Ling to attack, insisting that the people of Pu would join forces with the Wei troops and only a handful of rebels in Pu would be killed. However, perhaps because his own ministers were against such an offensive, Duke Ling ignored Confucius' advice. Furthermore, maybe because the Duke himself was losing interest in state affairs, he did not appoint Confucius to a post in his government. Confucius lamented, 'To be in office for just one year would satisfy me. In three years results would show.'[25] Although he may have remained in Wei for some time after this incident, he had given up hope by now of ever working for the Duke, and it seems that it was around this time that he was again tempted by a rebel who was planning to overthrow the government of a neighbouring state. In Jin, to the north-east of Wei, Bi Xi, governor of Zhongmou and steward of one of the great families of the state, had been attacked by another of the state's families. He fought back, using this assault to start his own rebellion, and invited Confucius to join him. Confucius was preparing to go to Bi Xi's aid when Zilu objected, once again acting as his teacher's conscience. He quoted Confucius' own words back at him: 'Master, in the past I heard you say, "A gentleman will not associate with those who are personally committing evil." Bi Xi is making use of his stronghold in Zhongmou to start a rebellion. How can you contemplate joining him?' Again Confucius conceded, replying, 'Indeed I said that. And yet what resists grinding is truly strong, what resists black dye is truly white. Am I a bitter gourd, good only to hang as decoration, but unfit to be eaten?'[26]

Such self-pity is rare from Confucius. Throughout the most arduous parts of their travels, he managed to maintain his confidence and belief in his Heavenly mission, and on many occasions succeeded in cheering up his followers, who may have been losing their faith. However, for a moment he shared with his trusted student and friend Zilu his despondency at his continued lack of professional success. Clearly he was frustrated that he performed a merely decorative function at all the courts where he stayed. Not one of the dukes whom he had advised had actually 'tasted' his advice, perhaps fearful that they might not be able to swallow or digest it. As a result, it seemed to him that all his years of study and all the knowledge he had accumulated and formed into a political philosophy had been wasted. His greatest fear – that of not being put to good use by a noble ruler – was apparently becoming a reality and it was painful for him to accept this.

Sima Qian suggests that after his 'bitter gourd' statement, Confucius threw himself into music, perhaps to soothe his soul and heal his wounds. He recounts that one day Confucius was playing the chimes in his home and a man carrying a wicker crate passed by his door. The man heard Confucius playing and declared, 'Poor fellow, playing the chimes! He is self-willed but does not know himself. It is useless to talk with him.' Such a statement implies that even the lowliest of characters in Wei were aware of Confucius' predicament, though they may not have been particularly sympathetic and seem to have had strong opinions about him. On another occasion, Confucius supposedly practised playing the lute for ten days without attempting anything new, demonstrating a somewhat obsessive approach to his own musical education. He had a music tutor called Shi Xiangzi, who encouraged him, telling him to go ahead and try a fresh piece. Confucius replied, 'I have learned the tune but not the technique,' and continued to practise. His teacher told him that he had mastered the technique and should go on to something different. Confucius then insisted, 'I have not yet caught the spirit.' Sometime later, his teacher said that he had indeed caught the spirit and advised him to move on. Confucius replied, 'I cannot yet visualise the man behind it,' but shortly afterwards declared, 'This is the work of a man who thought deeply

and seriously, one who saw far ahead and had a calm, lofty outlook. I see him now. He is dark and tall, with far-seeing eyes that
seem to command all the kingdoms around him. No one but King
Wen could have composed this music.' His teacher congratulated
him on his observations, revealing that the piece Confucius had
been working so hard to master was indeed the Lute Song of King
Wen. Although Confucius had perhaps been seeking escape from
his professional woes by immersing himself in the study of classical music, his fascination for this piece had brought him back to
one of his great cultural heroes, King Wen, a founder of the Zhou
dynasty and an inspiration for Confucius' political career.[27]

Shortly after this musical revelation, Confucius is said to have
composed a lute song of his own in honour of two virtuous ministers of the neighbouring state of Jin. Confucius planned to visit
Zhao Jianzi, the head of the powerful Zhao clan of Jin, in the hope
of finding work with him. However, when he reached the Yellow
River he heard the news that two of Zhao's ministers, Dou Mingdu
and Shun Hua, had been killed. Deeply shocked by their deaths,
he stared into the river and sighed, 'A grand sweep of water! But
I am not fated to cross it!' When his loyal student Zigong asked
him why not, he explained to him that these two men were of great
virtue. When Zhao Jianzi was rising to power he had insisted on
having the two wise ministers by his side, but now that he had
achieved it he had arranged for them to be killed. Confucius then
presented a more mystical explanation of why he could not now
proceed to Jin. 'I have heard that when you destroy unborn animals or kill young game, the unicorn will not come to the countryside; when you dredge and empty the ponds while fishing, the
dragon will not harmonise the *yin* and *yang*; when you destroy the
nest, the phoenix will not hover nearby. It follows that a gentleman
must take offence if one of his kind is injured. If the very birds and

beasts shun the unjust, how much more must I!' He turned back and stayed for a while in a small village, where he composed a lute song to mourn the two noble ministers who, like him, had been disregarded by those in power.[28]

His own relationship with Duke Ling of Wei remained complicated and strained. Confucius was not employed as an official adviser but, as we have already seen, the Duke still sought his advice. On one occasion the Duke apparently asked Confucius about warfare, and the latter replied, 'I know something about sacrificial vessels, but I have never studied military science.' Then, the next day, while they were conversing, the Duke looked up at some wild geese flying by and ignored Confucius. That act of disregard may well have been the last straw for Confucius, and he very likely considered the sight of the geese flying to be a bad omen, perhaps for the Duke. Confucius finally left Wei and returned to Chen in the south around 491 BC. Duke Ling died shortly afterwards.

Chen, Cai and She

Meanwhile, their home state of Lu was undergoing some significant political changes. Duke Ding of Lu had died in 494 BC, and a new Duke, Ai, had been appointed. The leader of the Jisun clan, feeling regretful about Confucius' departure from Lu, is said to have suggested to his own successor that he invite Confucius back and hire him as an adviser to Duke Ai. Apparently there was opposition to this idea among the other ministers of Lu, who felt that Confucius' resignation had been an embarrassment to the court and did not wish to risk another such departure. Under pressure from these ministers, the new Duke instead chose to hire one of Confucius' followers, Ran Qiu, as his adviser. Ran Qiu, who was probably travelling with Confucius at the time, eagerly accepted the appointment and began his service under Duke Ai. Confucius was undoubtedly disappointed and probably rather insulted by this turn of events, but was powerless to protest. Instead, one of his other students, Zigong, urged Ran Qiu to reinstate Confucius once he was installed in his new post. For reasons that are not clear, Ran Qiu did not do so immediately, leaving his teacher and fellow followers to wander for several more years.[29]

Although Confucius longed to leave Chen and return to Lu with Ran Qiu, his own pride forced him to await an invitation and he continued his peripatetic life away from home. It seems that he spent about a year in Chen. Then, according to Sima Qian, he stayed in the small neighbouring state of Cai for about three years. From Cai, he appears to have visited nearby She, a district that had once been part of Cai but was now under the jurisdiction of Chu. He was questioned by the Duke of She about good government. Confucius told him that the art of good government lies in 'attracting the people from far away and winning the hearts of those close by'.[30] Zilu apparently made a separate visit to She, and there he was asked by the Duke for his opinion of his teacher. When he told Confucius that he had been unable to give an opinion, Confucius said, 'Why didn't you tell him, "He is a man who never wearies of studying the truth, never tires of teaching others, but who in his eagerness forgets his hunger and in his joy forgets his bitter lot, not worrying that old age is creeping on"?' This charming and very revealing self-portrait helps us to understand why, even though he had moments of despondency during his days of wandering, he was able to continue travelling and teaching and hoping that he might be hired as an adviser. More than any government position or professional success, he valued the acquisition of knowledge and the sharing of this knowledge with others. It filled him with the joy necessary to forget his political failures and carry on.

While in She, Confucius became involved in a discussion with the governor about a criminal case that presented an interesting moral dilemma. It involved a man known as Upright Gong. Gong's father had apparently stolen a sheep, and when he was caught by the authorities, Gong bore witness against him. Confucius was not impressed by this man's actions and stated, 'Among my people, men of integrity do things differently: a father covers up for his son, and a son covers up for his father – and there is integrity in what they do.'[31] Confucius' response to the governor clearly indicates that he believed that one's loyalty lay first with one's family and then with the government. Probably because of Confucius' opinion of Upright Gong and his choice to turn his own father in, this dispute has become one of the most debated legal and moral cases in Chinese history.[32]

At around this point in Confucius' travels, he and his group are believed to have encountered several characters who may have been Daoist sages. These men typically renounced the world of cities, politics and human relationships in search of a more natural life that was closer to the *Dao*, the Way or force that animates the universe. Many of these recluses lived in the mountains or in rural settings, occasionally taking up farming to feed themselves. On the road from She back to Cai, Confucius and his party are said to have met two men who may have been such recluses, Changju and Jieni, ploughing the fields. Confucius instructed Zilu to ask the men for directions to the ford that they were planning to cross. When Zilu approached them, they asked him who the man driving the carriage was. When he told them that it was Confucius from the state of Lu, Changju replied, 'He should know where the ford is then.' Then, Jieni asked Zilu if he was one of Confucius' disciples, and Zilu replied that he was. Jieni's advice to Zilu was: 'The whole world goes its own way and who is to change it? Better, surely, to follow those who shun the world than one who only shuns certain men?'[33] With those words, the two men went on covering the seeds in their fields. When Zilu told Confucius what the men had said, he retorted, 'Birds and beasts are no company for men. If the world were on the right path I should not try to change it.'[34]

On another occasion while on the road, Zilu was alone and met an old man carrying a hoe and asked him if he had seen his master. The old man snapped at him with indignation, 'You who have never used your four limbs, who don't know the difference between the five grains – who is your master?' He then started weeding. When Zilu finally found Confucius and told him about the old man, Confucius replied that he must have been a recluse. They went back to the spot where he had been weeding, but he had disappeared.[35] Though very brief, these encounters between Confucius and his followers and the three Daoist recluses have been included in biographies of Confucius as a means of illustrating the key difference in approach between traditional Daoists and Confucianists. When human relationships became too difficult, Daoists would typically renounce society, while followers of Confucius would try to change society. The first two recluses were clearly mocking Confucius for rejecting his various employers but continuing to look for worthier men to work for, and advocated to Zilu their own approach of shunning all men. The old man, in turn, mocked Zilu for having no connection with the natural world and the earth. What kind of master, he implied, would fail to teach a student about living in nature?

Shortly after these two encounters Confucius and his group were travelling between Chen and Cai, and it was on this part of their journey that they met their greatest challenge. The large state of Wu attacked Chen, and the other large southern state of Chu came to Chen's defence, sending them troops that had been stationed nearby. The Chu leaders heard that Confucius was currently some-where between Chen and Cai and invited him to meet with them. According to Sima Qian, when the ministers of Chen and Cai heard this, they worried that Confucius was too familiar with the work-ings of their own two states and that if he were to be hired by the mighty state of Chu, his knowledge could be used against the two smaller states. So, Chen and Cai sent some troops to surround Confucius and his followers and make sure that they could not leave for Chu. Confucius and his group ran out of supplies and went without food for seven days.[36] Although they were on the verge of starvation and had nowhere to turn for help, Confucius merely played his lute and sang. It was at this point that Zilu chal-lenged Confucius to explain why a gentleman should find himself in such dire straits, and Confucius took advantage of their current predicament to teach them that it is at times, like these that one's true character is put to the test. When he asked his students why his teachings had not been adopted by a ruler, Yan Hui was the one who understood that they must never give up advocating the true, right way of their Master's teachings, no matter how much resistance they met. This was the sign of a real *junzi*, or gentleman.

After this important lesson, the group was somehow able to find help. Confucius apparently sent Zigong out to try to make his way to Chu, and the student was successful, persuading King Zhao to dis-patch troops to bring Confucius and his followers back to Chu. Chu was the largest and most powerful of the southern states that lay out-side Zhou territory. When they arrived in Chu, it was the first time they had left Zhou lands and found themselves among what they had presumably considered to be barbarians. Their stay there did not last long, however. King Zhao was on the verge of giving Confucius a large area of his domain to rule when his chief minister advised him that if he granted Confucius land, he and his entourage of highly able men might rise up and take over the whole empire themselves. King Zhao backed down and again Confucius was left without a position.

One day, when riding in his carriage, Confucius heard a man often described as the 'eccentric of Chu' singing to him as he passed the carriage:

> Ah, phoenix, phoenix,
> How powerless you are!
> Useless to blame what's done.
> Take thoughts for what's to come.
> Enough, enough!
> Today there is danger
> For those who guide the state.[37]

Confucius was startled by this song and climbed out of his carriage, hoping to find the singer. But the eccentric had run off. Perhaps Confucius was alarmed by the man's warning, or perhaps he was conscious of being too far from his home state. Again, he packed up his belongings, gathered his followers and made his way back north.

Final return to Wei

Again they landed in Wei. Confucius was already sixty-three years old and no doubt very tired of travelling. In Wei, according to Sima Qian, many of his students obtained government positions, while Zigong was called upon to resolve a conflict between Lu and the large southern state of Wu. Meanwhile, back home in Lu, his other former pupil Ran Qiu was successful in defeating the northern state of Qi in battle, and attributed his success to what he had learned from Confucius. He explained that his Master was someone who 'wants his actions to correspond to his principles. In applying his principles to govern the people he tries to carry out the wishes of the gods. This is what he wants, not to possess wealth to the value of a thousand wishes.' Apparently the chief minister of Lu, Ji Kangzi, was deeply impressed by this description of Confucius and asked, 'Can I ask him back?' Ran Qiu, aware of the past difficulties Confucius had met with other ministers, insisted, 'If you do, you must not let petty-minded men obstruct him.'[38] The minister agreed and sent an invitation to Confucius to return to Lu.

At that very moment one of the most powerful men in Wei was apparently eager for Confucius to stay there to advise him on military strategy, among other things. Although he was not interested or able, in his own opinion, to give military advice, Confucius must have been glad finally to be asked to serve in Wei after being largely ignored for so long. However, years of wandering from state to state during tense political times, as well as the numerous vain attempts to persuade rulers to follow his advice, must have worn Confucius down. Furthermore, as his later follower Mencius noted, the periods of time Confucius spent unemployed and far from home would have caused considerable anxiety for him as a gentleman. 'For a gentleman to lose his position is like a feudal lord losing his state.' Without a government post, a gentleman would have no land and without land he could have no sacrificial animals and vessels. Thus he would not be able to offer a sacrifice to his ancestors and host a feast for the living members of his family. For such a gentleman as Confucius, who was committed to honouring his ancestors, this must have been a source of distress.[39] Once the letter arrived from Duke Ai of Lu inviting Confucius to return, it was not hard for the Master to make his decision. He had been out of the state of Lu for fourteen years and it was time to go home.

8

The Final Years

Confucius returned to Lu in the winter of 484 BC. He had been invited back home by the Duke and Chief Counsellor of Lu, and they had sweetened the invitation with a large financial gift. This must have been a source of considerable satisfaction for Confucius after many years of feeling unappreciated in his home state. The two new rulers, Duke Ai and the Chief Counsellor, Ji Kangzi, had replaced Duke Ding and Ji Huanzi, who had been the cause of Confucius' departure from Lu fourteen years before, and these younger men no doubt perceived Confucius as a state elder, or *guolao*,[1] who possessed valuable political wisdom. He had travelled widely throughout the country and had experienced first-hand the political wrangling of the region, so he had acquired a unique knowledge of political affairs that would be a great benefit to any leader. Some of his wisdom was reflected in his two followers, Ran Qiu and Zigong, who now held prime government posts. Ran Qiu was employed as the Chief Steward of the mighty Jisun clan, who wielded the most power in Lu, and he had attributed his own recent victory against armies from the northern state of Qi to knowledge he had acquired from Confucius. Zigong, who was considered an expert in rites and diplomacy, had, as mentioned earlier, recently followed in his teacher's footsteps by using his diplomatic skills – rather than military might – to prevent a battle with (and likely defeat by) a powerful neighbouring state. At the age of sixty-nine, with the respect of his leaders and excellent connections in the government, Confucius finally seemed poised to become an important adviser to the Duke.

Indeed, Confucius is said to have provided both Duke Ai and Ji Kangzi with advice on several occasions. Duke Ai asked Confucius about good government, and Confucius replied, 'The art lies in choosing your ministers well.'² With this statement Confucius may well have been hinting to the Duke that he should hire him, but we know from his earlier comments about the Duke of Wei, who was a weak ruler but was surrounded by able advisers, that he genuinely thought that such men could offer great assistance to even the most incompetent ruler. On another occasion Ji Kangzi, who was not only Chief Counsellor but also head of the Jisun clan, sought his advice too. Confucius told him, 'If you use the straight in place of the crooked, the crooked will become straight.'³ Ji Kangzi was troubled by some cases of theft and asked Confucius for his opinion on the matter. Confucius responded, 'If you yourself were free from desire, they would not steal even if you paid them to do so,'⁴ suggesting to the minister the importance of leading by example. Ji Kangzi also asked Confucius, 'Suppose I were to kill the bad to help the good: how about that?' Confucius' reply is probably the most famous counsel he gave to any ruler or minister about the importance of leading from a position of exemplary morality: 'You are here to govern; what need is there to kill? If you desire what is good, the people will be good. The moral power of the gentleman is wind, the moral power of the common man is grass. Under the wind, the grass must bend.'⁵ Confucius chose such words in the hope of persuading the current Jisun leader to adopt a morally superior position as an administrator. Although Confucius probably did not know Ji Kangzi well enough to judge his personality, it seems likely that his advice to him may have been based on his own previous experience of the Jisun family, whom he considered to be far from straight in their political dealings and driven by a desire to enhance their own power.

It is possible the various words of advice that Confucius offered may not have sat well with the Duke or his Counsellor. Aside from these few exchanges with the leaders of Lu, Confucius seems to have had very little to do with the men in power after his return, and he was never actually offered an official post in the government. Nor was his counsel heeded on the rare occasion when he was consulted about government issues. At one point in 484 BC, when he was consulted about taxation, his opinion was ignored quite blatantly and, to his great dismay and outrage, the person who ignored it was Ran Qiu, his former student. That year the leaders of the Jisun family were considering imposing a land tax on their tenants, and Ran Qiu was dispatched to ask Confucius for his views on the subject. Confucius, who was passionately opposed to such a tax, knew that the Jisun family would not like his response so he refused to give it in an official capacity to Ran Qiu. Later, however, he privately advised Ran Qiu that the Jisun clan should not tax the people in addition to the grain that they had already produced and given to the government, since it was more than they could afford. He suggested that the Jisun follow the example of the early Zhou kings, who instituted the *fengjian* system of land distribution, in which land was shared and worked in a way that benefited both the ruler and his subjects.

We do not know what Ran Qiu himself thought of the proposed land tax, but it is clear from historical accounts of the period that he did not take his Master's advice. According to *The Spring and Autumn Annals*, in the spring of 483 BC the tax was imposed on the people and caused great hardship, made all the more devastating when the region was hit by three locust plagues over the next year and a half,[6] which were probably regarded as an indication of Heaven's displeasure at the suffering inflicted on the people. Not surprisingly, Confucius was furious at his former student for his lack of moral backbone. Did Ran Qiu not care about the plight of the farmers, or did he indeed care about them but was too cowardly to stand up to his employers and advise them to behave in a good and just manner? Either way, the steward demonstrated a lack of morality and was a failure in Confucius' eyes. In his anger Confucius proclaimed that Ran Qiu 'is no disciple of mine' and encouraged his other students to 'attack him openly to the beating of the drums'.[7] It was not typical of Confucius to endorse violence and he was probably speaking metaphorically here, but his response to Ran Qiu's lack of consideration for the struggling poor indicates the depth of his own compassion for their predicament.

Disappointed by the Duke and Chief Counsellor's lack of interest in his advice and in Ran Qiu's inability to question his employer's judgement, Confucius appears to have spent his last years just as he had spent many before, being largely ignored by the men in power who made the big decisions. Just as previously, he seems to have retreated into the realm of education, occupying himself again with teaching, research, writing and editing. More than ever, his reputation as a gentleman of great wisdom and worldly experience drew many young men to him, and he continued to educate them with undying enthusiasm. He had declared once while still in Chen that he wished to return to Lu to help 'our young men back home to shape their material',[8] and once back in Lu he posed the optimistic question, 'How do we know that the generations to come will not be the equal of the present?'[9] It seems that although he may have given up trying to teach current rulers and administrators how to be virtuous leaders, he still held great hope for the younger generations. If, by teaching them about history, rituals and music, he could show them how to be good moral rulers and administrators, he might succeed in having a positive influence on future governments.

A new student, Zizhang (503–447 BC), was one of the smartest and most inquisitive of Confucius' followers, and was surely a joy for Confucius to teach in his later years. He bombarded his Master with challenging questions about virtue, moral judgement and self-cultivation, pushing Confucius in turn to form some of his most astute observations about human nature, education and morality. For instance, when Zizhang requested Confucius' definition of discernment or clear-sightedness, the Master responded, 'He who is soaked in slander and deafened with denunciations, and still does not waver, may be called clear-sighted. Actually he may also be called farsighted.'[10] He also asked Confucius how to acquire moral power and how to know when one's judgement is clouded or incoherent. His Master explained, 'Put loyalty and faith above everything, and follow justice. That is how one accumulates moral power. When you love someone, you wish him to live; when you hate someone, you wish him to die. Now, if you simultaneously wish him to live and die, this is an instance of incoherence.'[11]

However, Zizhang apparently made no secret of his ambition to attain a high-level government position, and his intensity as a student was motivated more by ambition than an urge to cultivate his moral character. Surprisingly, this does not seem to have bothered his teacher, and in fact Confucius gave him very specific advice about how to succeed in government: 'Collect much information, put aside what is doubtful, repeat cautiously the rest; then you will seldom say something wrong. Make many observations, leave aside what is suspect, apply cautiously the rest; then you will seldom have cause for regret. With few mistakes in what you say and few regrets for what you do, your career is made.'[12] It seems that Confucius had decided that if his clever student was indeed destined to become a government official, it was his job to make sure that Zizhang went into government armed with the finest moral equipment possible. This is no doubt what he was referring to as 'shaping the material' of the young men of Lu. Zizhang apparently appreciated Confucius' wisdom and went so far as to write down his teacher's words on his sash, as if to ensure that his Master's teachings accompanied him wherever he went to keep him in check.[13]

Another of Confucius' later students, Zixia (506–443 BC), was also exceptional, and in *The Analects* he is noted for his cultural abilities.[14] Like Zizhang, Zixia pursued a government career and became the warden of Jufu. He too asked Confucius for political advice, to which the Master replied, 'Do not try to hurry things. Ignore petty advantages. If you hurry things, you will not reach your goal. If you pursue petty advantages, larger enterprises will not come to fruition.'[15] It appears that Zixia was also a devoted scholar with a particular interest in literature. On one occasion he asked Confucius about a stanza in a poem in *The Book of Songs*, and his incisive interpretation of a line of the poem earned from Confucius the exclamation, 'Ah, you really opened my eyes! It is only with you that one can discuss the *Poems*!'[16] What seems more important to note about Zixia, however, is that, according to *The Analects*, Zixia was one of the students who attempted to preserve and interpret Confucius' teachings after his Master died. Several references are made in *The Analects* to Zixia's disciples and followers and many of the sayings quoted in the final chapters about correct moral behaviour and attitudes may seem very similar to words of Confucius, but are attributed to Zixia.[17]

Even in his final years as a teacher, it seems that Confucius was no less strict with Zizhang and Zixia than he was with his earlier students, and he held them to extremely high standards. On one occasion his older follower Zigong is said to have asked him about these two, 'Which is better: Zizhang or Zixia?' When Confucius replied 'Zizhang overshoots and Zixia falls short,' Zigong then said, 'Then Zizhang must be better?', to which Confucius said, 'Both miss the mark.'[18] Zizhang was brilliant but not morally focused, while Zixia was a hard-working and meticulous scholar but perhaps did not reflect adequately on what he had learned. Nonetheless, Confucius undoubtedly appreciated both students for the intellectual stimulation they provided him with in his late sixties and early seventies, as well as for the hope they gave him for the future of the state of Lu.

Alongside teaching, Confucius is often said to have spent his final years working on the major texts that have long been attributed to him. According to early historians, because of the decline in Zhou power in Confucius' time, the rites and music of the kingdom had been neglected and its historical records were in disarray, and to remedy this Confucius compiled both *The Book of History* and *The Book of Rites*. They also claimed that he compiled *The Book of Songs* by reviewing over three thousand ancient songs; he 'rejected those which were repetitious and retained those which had moral value' and then 'set right the music and arranged the odes and hymns in the proper order'.[19] It is likely that Confucius did indeed spend his last years studying history, ritual and song, as he had throughout his life, but his exact role in the compilation of *The Book of History*, *Book of Rites* and *Book of Songs* has not yet been determined; and although many of his teachings were based on these three great texts, it is more probable that he was a proponent of and commentator on these works than their actual author, compiler or editor.[20]

A fourth text that Confucius is traditionally said to have worked on at this time is *The Spring and Autumn Annals*, the official chronicle of the state of Lu covering the period from 722 to 481 BC. This text is the earliest surviving Chinese historical text to be arranged in a year-by-year format. It is short and concisely written, but is only really understandable via the various commentaries that have been appended to it, including most famously the *Zuo Commentary (Zuo Zhuan)*, said to be the work of the court writer Zuo Qiuming around the late fourth century BC. Confucius is said to have based *The Annals* on the existing historical records of the reigns of twelve rulers of Lu, from that of Duke Yin down to the fourteenth year of the reign of the current Duke Ai. The text focuses on the state of Lu, but it supposedly has as its guiding principle the spirit of the Three Dynasties (the Xia, Shang and Zhou); and, according to Sima Qian, when this principle is carried out, 'all traitors and evil-doers in the world must tremble.'[21] Confucius supposedly chose to record certain events and omit others and prophesied that 'It is these annals by which later men will know me and it is these annals which will make men condemn me.'[22]

It would certainly have made sense for Duke Ai of Lu to commission Confucius, with his great knowledge of the past, both ancient and recent, to document the history of the state, and since both Sima Qian and Mencius (372–289 BC), a later philosopher and follower of Confucius, claimed that Confucius was the author of this work, he has for many centuries been thus accredited. However, as with the three other books, there is no evidence that this is so. Few modern scholars believe that he had anything to do with the text and they generally attribute its composition to a number of state chroniclers. Yet, as a historian himself, he was surely aware that such a work was being compiled. It is not hard to imagine though, that Duke Ai, who had chosen not to use Confucius as a political adviser, also overlooked the senior scholar when he appointed an official court historian.

A fifth text that is also associated with Confucius' final years is *The Book of Changes*, a mystical work which contains commentaries on sixty-four magical hexagrams that are used in divination to provide answers to all aspects of life. Even though *The Book of Changes* has traditionally been more closely associated with Daoism, with its emphasis on the forces that animate the universe and our relationship with them, from the time of Confucius onwards the work has also been grouped with the four books mentioned to make up the Five Classics, a corpus of texts that are considered to form the basis of Confucian teachings. This is because, in the final years of his life, Confucius apparently 'loved to study *The Book of Changes*, the order of the hexagrams, definitions, appendices, interpretations, explanations and commentaries'. In fact, he supposedly spent so much time reading it that 'the leather thongs binding the wooden strips wore out three times', and his fascination with it drove him to proclaim, 'Give me a few more years and I shall become quite proficient!'[23] Over the centuries some biographers have credited Confucius with editing and writing commentaries on this work, but such claims do not seem to be supported by any historical evidence.[24]

Nonetheless, even if he did not contribute edits or commentaries to the book itself, it may well be true that Confucius was intrigued by this mystical work in his old age. His students apparently found this puzzling, as it seemed to contradict his teachings. From early records it appears that 'the subjects on which he did not talk were: extraordinary things, feats of strength, political disorders, and the supernatural',[25] and it is noted in *The Analects* that Confucius taught his students to 'respect ghosts and gods, but keep them at a distance'.[26] In addition, Zigong once remarked, 'We can hear the master's views concerning culture, but he does not tell us anything about Nature and Fate.'[27] When he observed Confucius poring over *The Book of Changes*, Zigong is said to have reminded him that he had taught his students that an interest in spiritualism displayed a loss of virtue and that a desire to know the future led to divination. He asked his teacher why he was now so drawn to such things. Confucius argued that the appeal of *The Book of Changes* was merely academic. He was not trying to see the future but to read the words of wisdom in the text.[28]

Although traditional accounts have Confucius denying any interest in the supernatural, when he was seventy he is said to have had an encounter with a creature that does not exist in this world and he recognised it too well for a practical person who dwells only in the secular realm. In 481 BC, the fourteenth year of the reign of Duke Ai, Confucius was summoned by representatives of the Duke to the western part of Lu to give his advice on an unusual discovery. Some nobles had been hunting in the area and had captured a mysterious animal which they considered to be somewhat inauspicious. Confucius, who was respected for his broad knowledge, was asked what it might be and, on seeing it, he exclaimed, 'This is a *qilin*! ... All is over with me! ... My way has come to an end!'[29] It will be remembered that before she bore him, Confucius' mother had had a dream in which she was visited by five gods who brought with them a *qilin*. In her dream she tied a ribbon around the horn of the beast. The appearance of this creature was said to portend the arrival of a truly great and virtuous individual. The beast that Confucius encountered, according to some accounts, also had a ribbon tied around its horn, suggesting that it was bringing a message specifically to Confucius. Whether or not this beast wore a ribbon, Confucius was shocked to see it, as it was to him a sign that he was soon to die. With the realisation that his end was near, he lamented to the students who were with him that his Way had not gained popularity because no one but Heaven understood him. He confided to them that, 'What a gentleman dreads is to die before his name is known ... How shall I make myself known to later ages?'[30]

Shortly after this incident Confucius became seriously ill, and it seemed that the omen of the *qilin* might be true. He was so sick that Duke Ai decided to pay him a visit. Despite his weak state, Confucius chose to dress in his finest court robes and, even though he appeared to be close to death, he made sure to follow protocol by lying on his bed with his head facing east to greet his lord.[31] Confucius recovered from this illness, but in the last couple of years of his life, he witnessed the deaths of some of his closest friends and family members. At some time around 483 BC his son Boyu and his wife had a son, Zisi, who grew up to be a philosopher who closely followed his grandfather's teachings. However, Boyu died shortly after the birth of his son, meaning that Zisi, like Confucius, grew up not knowing his own father, a fact that was no doubt very sad for his grandfather, though there may have been some consolation that his son had had a son who could continue to honour the family ancestors. Confucius made sure that Boyu was buried according to protocol, with a very humble coffin and rites that befitted his status.

Very soon after his son's death, Confucius received word that his old friend Zilu was dead. He had been employed as a minister in Wei, and the court of Wei had again become embroiled in scandal. The Duke of Wei's widowed sister had taken a servant as a lover and had urged the man to organise a coup in order to reinstate a banished heir. Zilu was loyal to his lord, the Duke, and tried to take him to safety in Lu, but was killed while attempting to defend him in a fight at the palace.[32] Although Confucius had predicted that Zilu, who was impetuous and staunchly loyal, would die a violent death, he was nonetheless shocked and saddened to lose one of his oldest and most loyal disciples – one who had always been there to help him from straying from his own noble path.

Around the same time, Confucius was devastated by the death of his favourite pupil, Yan Hui, who had not yet reached his fortieth birthday. To Confucius, Yan Hui had always seemed the closest to truly understanding his teachings, since he listened and absorbed his Master's words very carefully and was of a moral character that was purer than that of anyone else he knew.[33] On hearing of Yan Hui's death, Confucius cried out, 'Alas! Heaven is destroying me! Heaven is destroying me!'[34] He had witnessed the *qilin* who portended his own death, and now the one student who he believed could carry his teachings to the next generation was dead. He was now convinced that his Way would not survive after his own death.[35]

He wailed wildly with grief at Yan Hui's passing, and although his students thought his strong emotional outburst unfitting, Confucius insisted that such grief was appropriate for such a great man. Perhaps too, he was mourning the end of his teachings.[36]

His other students, perhaps in an attempt to honour Yan Hui in a way that befitted his rank among Confucius' students, decided to give him a grand burial. Confucius forbade them, saying that this was not the right protocol for a student. The students ignored their Master's objections and organised an ostentatious funeral. Confucius was furious, saying, 'Yan Hui treated me as his father, and yet I was not given the chance to treat him as my son. This is not my fault, but yours, my friends.'[37] Treating him like his son would have meant giving him a modest funeral in accordance with his status, just like the one he had given his real son, Boyu. Confucius was angry that his students had deprived him of this honour for his beloved student.

Yan Hui's death was surely a difficult time, not only for Confucius but for his other students too. To hear him lament that now there would be no one to carry on his teachings to the next generation was probably painful for the most devoted of his disciples, who had worked hard to understand and follow their Master's doctrines. It seems that Confucius underestimated his other students' ability to absorb, apply and advocate his Way, since many of them did go on to be scholars and teachers of his philosophy. It was their followers in turn who were successful in having his teachings recognised by the rulers of the land and ultimately incorporated into the government and educational systems. Indeed, his own grandson, Zisi, became a well respected teacher; and one of his students was Mencius, a great proponent of Confucius' beliefs and an outstanding philosopher in his own right.

Nonetheless, after Yan Hui's death Confucius felt that he now had very little to live for. He was in his seventies, he believed that he had lost his potential successor, and he had not succeeded in convincing his own lord of the importance and virtue of his Way. Although he had cried out that Heaven was destroying him, he may well also have felt that he had failed Heaven in his mission to spread the true, virtuous Way among the people of his land. In the spring of 479 BC, Confucius fell ill again. The nature of his illness is not clear, but he was apparently feisty and challenging to his students even in his last days. Zigong, who remained devoted to Confucius, may have become his attendant in his final years. One day, when he went to see him, his Master was pacing by the door with a stick and demanded, 'Why have you come so late?' After he had calmed down, he quoted a poem to Zigong:

Mount Tai crumbles,
The great beam breaks,
The wise man withers away.[38]

He tearfully told Zigong that he had dreamed that he was sitting before offerings between two pillars, a vision that Zigong, who had learned much about ritual from Confucius, recognised. Members of the Shang dynasty, from which Confucius supposedly descended, laid out the corpses of their dead between two pillars. Confucius was dreaming about his own imminent death. Then, with Zigong by his side, he uttered his final words, which were filled with regret and disappointment: 'No intelligent monarch arises; there is not one in the kingdom that will make me his master. My time has come to die.[39] He took to his bed and, within seven days, Confucius was dead. He was seventy-three years old.

On hearing of his death, Duke Ai is said to have lamented, 'Kind Heaven had no pity on me and would not spare this grand old man. I am left alone in the world, full of grief and sorrow. Oh, Master, to whom shall I look for guidance now?' Such an outburst of emotion was too little too late for Confucius' followers. Zigong, who had witnessed Confucius' final lament that he had not been used well by his lord, was wary of the Duke's supposed remorse, and commented cynically, 'Not to employ the master during his lifetime but to mourn him after his death runs counter to true ceremony, while the description "alone in the world" does not befit a duke.'[40]

Confucius was buried by a river north of the capital of Lu. Many of his followers mourned him for the customary three-year period. Zigong, loyal even after his Master's death, built a hut next to the grave and continued to mourn for another three years. Other students left the area, but it is said that more than a hundred of his former pupils settled near their Master's grave, and so the locals named the district Confucius Village. Having learned well from their Master about performing the correct rituals for the dead, his followers, and many other locals, continued to sacrifice at his grave. For hundreds of years his grave and his home, which was soon turned into a temple, have been sites of pilgrimage for those who wish to honour the man who has been known for centuries in China as the 'Supreme Sage.'

CONCLUSION

The Legacy of Confucius and His Teachings

'A gentleman worries lest he might disappear from this world without having made a name for himself.'[1]

For most of his long life, Confucius managed to retain an unshakeable faith in his political destiny. In his final years, however, he began to realise that he would not be given the chance to use his philosophy to heal the troubles of the land, and he began to contemplate the possibility that his life's work might have been in vain. It seems likely that the above words about the plight of a gentleman referred to his own predicament as a man who strove to put morality and virtue before all else but could not convince rulers of its importance. At his death, he had not succeeded in making a name for himself in government; instead, his confidence in his beliefs had probably alienated him from those in power in Lu and abroad. Consequently, his supposed final poem to his student Zigong, which refers to mountains crumbling and a wise man withering away, reflects his feelings of failure and desolation. He seemed certain that his philosophy might die with him. Apparently, although he had long believed in his own Heavenly mission, he did not trust in the strength of his teachings to endure without him or in the ability of his own followers, whom he had spent a lifetime training, to transmit his teachings for him. He underestimated both.

After his death, many of his students continued to practise and pass on the Way of Confucius. Some attained government positions and gradually incorporated aspects of his teachings into government. Others became scholars and taught his philosophy to younger students who, like themselves years before, yearned to study culture, history and rites and to cultivate their moral characters. It is likely that the early generations of followers of Confucius simply referred to his philosophy as 'the Way', as Confucius had, but eventually it was given the name *Rujia* (literally, 'the School of the Scholars'), *Ruxue* ('the Study of the Scholars'), or *Rujiao* ('the Teachings of the Scholars'). None of these terms included his name, but occasionally his philosophy is referred to as *Kongjiao*, or 'the Teaching of Confucius'. These terms have different connotations in Chinese, some more secular, some more religious. The ending *jia*, meaning family or house, denotes a school of thought and appears in other philosophies, such as *fajia*, or Legalism. The ending *xue*, meaning study, is used similarly to the English ending '-ology' to refer to sciences, such as *jingjixue*, meaning 'economics', and *shengwuxue*, meaning 'biology'. The term *jiao* means teach or educate, but forms the names of religions such as *Huijiao* for Islam and *Jidujiao* for Christianity. In the West the philosophy is typically named after Confucius, and the English name 'Confucianism', for example, has certainly fuelled the belief that his teachings are a religion similar to Buddhism, Hinduism or Judaism.

Not surprisingly, there is much debate in China about whether Confucianism is a philosophy, an ideology or a religion. There is not enough space here to tackle such a complex and provocative question.[2] It is probably safe to say, though, that his teachings, as they have evolved over the centuries, contain elements of all of the above categories. It is also worth noting that in East Asia the lines between religions and philosophies have traditionally, been more blurred, perhaps, than in the Western world. The question 'Is Confucianism a religion?' has not traditionally been asked there. Generally, followers of Confucius' teachings have considered Confucianism to be a moral code that provides guidance on both a social and a political level, and many followers of his teachings are also Buddhists or Christians. Yet, at times, the same people might also have prayed at Confucian temples and made offerings to statues of Confucius, for example for success in examinations. Whatever we choose to call the teachings of Confucius,[3] his early followers believed them to contain the key to social and political harmony and they endeavoured to pass them on to successive generations, despite significant resistance and opposition. Their determination certainly bore fruit. Over the centuries, Confucianism flourished within China and eventually evolved into a more complex philosophy that included metaphysical and mystical aspects. It then spread throughout East Asia and to parts of South-east Asia, and accompanied Chinese communities as they settled in other parts of the world. This chapter will examine the legacy and impact of Confucius and Confucianism in these areas and beyond.

Confucianism in China

The later part of the Eastern Zhou period, known as the Warring States period (476–221 BC), was even more unstable and violent than the early Zhou period when Confucius had lived. Six or seven of the larger states had swallowed up their smaller neighbours and were at war with each other for supremacy in the region. Probably because of this unrest, this was also a time of remarkable intellectual and philosophical activity. Philosophers from the so-called 'Hundred Schools of Thought' – including Confucianism, Daoism and Legalism – laid out their theories about human nature, presented ideas for restoring harmony and competed passionately with each other for the attention and patronage of rulers. Some thinkers developed new philosophies to tackle life's big questions, while others interpreted or elaborated upon the teachings of early thinkers, including Confucius. Two in particular, Mencius and Xunzi, were critical in propagating and revitalising Confucius' teachings during this turbulent age.

Mengzi, known in English as Mencius (372–289 BC), played an extremely important role in consolidating Confucius' doctrines and defending them against the many rival schools of thought. Mencius grew up close to Confucius' birthplace and is believed to have studied under Confucius' grandson, Zisi. He has been regarded by many Confucians as the 'Second Sage', the most important Confucian thinker after Confucius himself. He embraced Confucius' pursuit of a moral, virtuous life and elaborated upon Confucius' beliefs in two significant ways. Most importantly, he devoted much of his teachings to the discussion of human nature, arguing that humans are essentially good. He proposed that, just as the society of their age was a perversion and corruption of an earlier and perfect age (Confucius' golden age of the Western Zhou), the characters of most people had also been distorted from their original state of goodness. Because all human beings have an essentially kind and moral disposition, they can recover their virtue. Education for Mencius was not about how to get 'good feelings', as Confucius taught, but about how to keep the ones already present in people's characters.[4] Mencius believed that by cultivating the four kinds of predispositions that exist in all human hearts or minds –

commiseration, a sense of shame, a reverential attitude towards others and a sense of right and wrong – all people have the ability to attain the four most important ethical attributes: *ren* (benevolence, humanity), *li* (observance of rites), *yi* (righteousness), and *zhi* (wisdom).

A second area in which Mencius expanded on Confucius was the concept of the benevolent ruler. Like Confucius, he taught that a ruler must possess *ren*, or benevolence, but also insisted that he exercise a strong sense of *yi*, righteousness or duty, arguing that a ruler who was not righteous towards his people should forfeit his entitlement to rule. 'A king,' he claimed, 'is he who gives expression of his humanity through virtuous conduct.'[5] Only if a ruler treats his people with dignity and puts their economic welfare first can he be become a true king. His criteria for kingship are described at several points in the *Mencius*: 'When the aged wear silk and eat meat and the common people are free from hunger and cold, never has the lord of such people failed to become king.'[6] Like Confucius, Mencius spent much of his life travelling from state to state trying to offer advice to leaders to reform, but he was even less successful than Confucius in persuading the premiers of the day to focus on developing their moral character and taking care of their people. He lived in an even more politically turbulent time than Confucius had, and the rulers of the powerful states of the region were generally less interested in keeping their people fed than in defending or expanding their own territory. They had little time for Mencius. Like his predecessor, he ended his days teaching and writing. His interpretation of Confucius' teachings has been considered the orthodox version of Confucianism by many later Confucians, especially the Neo-Confucians of the Song dynasty. The *Mencius*, the book of his teachings that was probably compiled by his students, is one of the core texts of Confucianism.

The third great early thinker of Confucianism was Xunzi (c. 312–230 BC). Little is known about his early life, but in his fifties he became a high official in the state of Qi and later travelled south to occupy a similar position in Chu. A student of Confucius, he opposed many of the superstitions of the day and argued for a more rational view of the universe and of people and, like Confucius and Mencius, he too emphasised the importance of education to cultivate the self. Where his teachings diverge most remarkably from those of Mencius is in his description of the human character. Unlike Mencius, who believed that human nature is essentially good and that evil is caused by abusing or neglecting this innate goodness, Xunzi argued that human nature is essentially evil, and that goodness is the result of education. All that is good in society, he believed, comes from training and restraining the crude animal nature of humans. 'Crooked wood needs to undergo steaming and bending by the carpenter's tools. Only then is it straight ... Now the original nature of man is evil, so he must submit himself to teachers and laws before he can be just.'[7]

Regarding government, Xunzi also valued the importance of a good and virtuous ruler, but because of his belief in the essential evil of human nature he also advocated a system of rewards and punishments to help keep the people in order. Here he clearly strayed from the teachings of both Confucius and Mencius, but his approach, which was often considered to be more realistic or pragmatic than those of the two earlier sages, gained him a number of followers. However, two of his most famous students, Li Si and Han Feizi, went on to become staunch anti-Confucianists under Qin Shi Huang, the warlord who finally unified the Warring States in the third century BC. Their participation in the near-eradication of the teachings of Confucius greatly damaged Xunzi's reputation and legacy as a Confucianist.

The period of the Warring States ended in 221 BC, when the king of Qin conquered the other large states, unified the region and proclaimed himself Qin Shi Huang Di, 'The First Emperor of Qin'. Confucius had hoped for the restoration of peace and unity, but Qin Shi Huang Di (259–210 BC) was far from Confucius' ideal gentleman-ruler and his regime is typically described as totalitarian. Although he is responsible for such astounding cultural achievements as the completion of the Great Wall, which protected the country from northern invasions, and the construction of road and canal networks that developed trade and transportation, the human cost was high, as many of these projects were undertaken using slave labour and paid for by high taxes on farmers. He also ordered the standardisation of script, coinage, weights and measures, which improved communication within the vast empire. However, in an attempt to monopolise and control knowledge and prevent opposition to his rule, he destroyed books that he believed to be threatening, including the works of Confucius, and put to death scholars whose teachings he considered dangerous. (He kept copies of the Confucian texts in the Imperial Library for government use, but these were destroyed during the collapse of the Qin dynasty when the library was burned down.)

The philosophy the First Emperor adopted for his rule was known as Legalism, or the School of Law, a doctrine that one of Xunzi's students, Han Feizi (c. 280–233 BC), developed from Xunzi's belief that humans are essentially evil. Whereas Xunzi was optimistic that people could be trained to become good, the Legalist School argued that government, rules and regulations were necessary to keep their behaviour in check. Qin Shi Huang Di used this philosophy to dismantle the old state feudal system and establish absolute central rule with an exhaustive set of laws and severe punishments. The people were expected to be frugal and obedient and to serve the state in times of war and peace. Xunzi's other famous student, Li Si (c. 280–208 BC), was the Qin emperor's prime minister, and was central to overseeing the state's Legalist policies, including the persecution of Confucianism and any other philosophies that opposed Legalism. Although Li Si himself was a scholar and renowned calligrapher, he was the one who suggested the burning of books and execution of scholars and intellectuals deemed to be politically threatening. According to Sima Qian, Li Si recommended that even 'those who dare to talk to each other about *The Book of Songs* and *The Book of History* should be executed and their bodies exposed in the market place'.[8] During this period followers of Confucius' teachings kept a low profile, but despite the ban on Confucian texts some books were hidden away and survived the burnings.

The Qin dynasty was short-lived and collapsed under the reign of its second emperor in 207 BC. It was followed by the Han dynasty (206 BC–AD 220), which inherited the Qin legacy of a huge empire with a centralised state. Fortunately for Confucianism and other philosophical schools, Han rulers did not attempt to stamp out intellectual activity among the people. Instead, this was a period of great scholarly recovery and growth in China, and although Legalism was still prominent, Daoism and eventually Buddhism became increasing prominent. Confucianism in particular flourished and finally, under the seventh Han ruler, Emperor Wudi (156–87 BC, r. 140–87 BC), gained the imperial patronage that Confucius had hoped for. In 135 BC, following the death of Wudi's grandmother, the Grand Dowager Empress Dou, who was a devoted Daoist and a powerful force at court, Confucianism rose in influence to become the dominant imperial philosophy. Confucian texts (and those associated with him, such as *The Book of Songs* and *The Book of History* that had been particularly singled out by Li Si) were required reading for civil service examinations. Now, government positions were not only accessible to those of rank, but to any man who could show in these examinations that he had mastered the classical texts and absorbed Confucius' ideas about morality and ethical government. Eventually, by the end of the Han dynasty, a class of scholar officials grew to dominate the entire Chinese social system, further bolstering the importance of Confucian studies for centuries to come.

It was during this period also that Confucianism began to take on a cosmic character. Although Confucius himself likely believed in the concept that rulers require a Heavenly Mandate to govern, his teachings did not emphasise the relationship between human behaviour and natural occurrences. His follower Xunzi was the first Confucianist to stress the connection between human virtue and cosmic stability, claiming, 'Heaven operates with constant regularity ... respond to it with good government and blessings will result; respond to it with misgovernment and misfortune will result.'[9] A century after him, under the Han dynasty, many Confucianists embraced Xunzi's theory that correct moral behaviour was related to the workings of the universe. At this time, much attention was paid by philosophers to the problems of evil, which they believed to be a matter of the natural order rather than theology, ethics or psychology.[10] They sought to understand the cause of calamities such as earthquakes or floods that wrought havoc on all people, good or bad. Han Confucianists joined in the debate, proposing that humans played a part.[11] They believed that Heaven watched over them like a beneficent father, but when it noticed that its servant or son, namely the emperor, was mismanaging human affairs and disturbing the social order on earth it would cause a disruption of the natural, cosmic order, with an earthquake or other catastrophe. Such a theory afforded a legitimate basis for imperial government, reminiscent of the Shang and Zhou dynasty belief that kings were Sons of Heaven. At the same time, it required the emperor to be morally responsible to his people or suffer the punishment of Heaven.[12]

Although state support during the Han dynasty established the Confucian classics as the basis of the government examination system and the core of the educational curriculum, Confucianism could not maintain the same level of popularity after the collapse of the Han. During the centuries of chaos that followed the Han, and even under the Tang dynasty (AD 618–906), which united China and restored peace and great prosperity, Confucianism was in many ways eclipsed by Daoism and Buddhism, which received considerable royal patronage and won a significant following among the general populace. Under the Tang, Confucianism remained the accepted political philosophy, and the civil service examination system, which was based on Confucius' teachings, became even more highly organised and well administered than before. The doctrines of Confucius also served as a general code of ethics, and most people followed them at home within the family structure and at work, especially in the imperial government. Confucian scholars continued to study and transmit his teachings, and many Confucian temples were erected throughout the empire as places to revere his principles. However, there were few Confucianists, that is, people who followed Confucius as a distinct creed that set them apart from others,[13] and much of the population turned to Buddhism or Daoism to satisfy many of their spiritual needs. Towards the end of the period, in the ninth century, some scholars, including Han Yu (786–824), challenged Daoism and Buddhism and championed Confucianism, but their voices were not heard until later.

It was during the Song dynasty (960–1279) that Confucianism again experienced a major revival. The main figure in this renaissance was the philosopher Zhu Xi (1130–1200), a follower of Confucius who was also well versed in Buddhist and Daoist philosophy. He and other Song Confucianists examined the nature of the soul and the relation of the individual to the cosmos, concepts that were important in Buddhism and Daoism but had not yet been explored within Confucianism. Under these philosophers, Confucianism evolved into a more metaphysical philosophy, in which every individual's morality was connected to a universal principle known as *li* (written with the character 理, and not to be confused with *li*, meaning ritual, which is written with the character 禮). Zhu Xi maintained that 'The Way [*li*] is identical with the nature of man and things and their nature is identical with the Way.'[14] He taught that all things in the universe, including objects and people, are brought into being by the union of two aspects of reality: *li*, which can be translated as rational principle (or law), and *qi*, vital (or physical, material) force. According to Zhu Xi, the source and sum of all *li* is the Great Ultimate, or *Taiji*, a supreme creative principle similar to, though not exactly the same as, the *Dao* of Daoism. Every physical object and every person has its own *li* (something like the soul, mind, or spirit) and is therefore metaphysically connected with the *Taiji*. This *li* is pure, meaning that human nature is essentially good, but it is sheathed in matter or *qi*, so action is needed to restore its purity. For Zhu Xi, because *li* is all around us, the most effective way to purify one's *li* was to study the *li* in the world using a form of observational science known in Chinese as *gewu*, literally the 'investigation of things'. This rational study of the world was to be given precedence over any sort of emotional approach to questions of right and wrong.

The importance of *li* in this new form of Confucianism gave the movement its Chinese name, *lixue*, literally 'the study of *li*'. In the West we know it as Neo-Confucianism. It is the form of Confucianism that was most widely embraced both in China and in other parts of East Asia following the Song dynasty. Zhu Xi further increased the influence of Confucianism both in China and beyond by compiling the Confucian canon as it exists today. He selected what he considered to be the most important texts of Confucianism and codified the canon of *Four Books* (*The Great Learning*, *Doctrine of the Mean*, *The Analects of Confucius* and *Mencius*) which, in the subsequent Ming and Qing dynasties, were made the core of the official curriculum for the civil service examinations and which were adopted as the key texts of Confucianism when the philosophy spread to Korea, Japan and Vietnam.[15]

During the Ming dynasty (1368–1644), Neo-Confucianism was adopted by the government as the state ideology and generally followed by Confucian scholars of the period. However, although Confucianists largely agreed with Zhu Xi about the importance of *li*, some disagreed on how to purify it. One important Confucianist thinker of the era, Wang Yangming (1472–1529), suggested that since *li* is present in everything, it is also within our own hearts, so we should look inward by meditating in order to understand the difference between good and evil. Because of his emphasis on the cultivation of the mind-heart, Wang's teaching was referred to as *xinxue*, or 'teaching of the mind-heart', as opposed to Zhu's *lixue*, or 'teaching of principle'. Wang also believed that anyone, regardless of socio-economic status or background, had the potential to become as wise as the ancient sages, and that a peasant who had learned from his many experiences in the natural world could become wiser than a court official who had studied Confucian texts but not experienced real life.[16] He and other like-minded Confucians reached out to the lower classes and even encouraged women to become educated. Such thinking was considered dangerous by conservative Confucianists within the government, who pushed for a return to orthodox Confucian ethics.

Although the Qing dynasty (1644–1911) was established by the non-Chinese Manchu, many of the Ming governmental and cultural institutions were preserved, including the Confucian-based legislative and educational systems. Despite the continued support for Confucianism, there was a movement among Confucian scholars of the seventeenth to the nineteenth centuries away from the metaphysical Neo-Confucianism of Zhu Xi and Wang Yangming and back to the earlier Confucianism of the Han dynasty. Certain Qing Confucianists, including Gu Yanwu (1613–82) and Dai Zhen (1724–77), argued that the Neo-Confucianists had distorted the original teachings of Confucius, tainting them with Buddhist and Daoist ideas. They also believed that human emotions such as desire were not obstacles to rational investigation, as the Neo-Confucians had taught, but an integral part of the human experience. Adopting an approach that was known as *hanxue*, or 'Han Teaching', or *kaozhengxue*, 'Evidential Research Learning', these scholars closely examined the writings of Han Confucians, who they believed were closer both in time and thinking to Confucius, and they painstakingly dissected the language of Confucian classics and other ancient texts in an attempt to trace the true words of Confucius.[17]

In the late nineteenth century, pressure by Western cultures to open up to trade and diplomacy contributed to the collapse of the last dynasty. Despite the efforts of activists such as Kang Youwei (1858–1927) a Confucian scholar and political thinker who inspired the 1898 reform movement that aimed to preserve Chinese values in the face of Westernization, Western influence permeated Chinese culture, and the Chinese increasingly perceived their own traditions as backward. In mainland China during the twentieth century, particularly under Mao during the Cultural Revolution, Confucius was declared a symbol of China's imperial and feudal past and thus an enemy of the people and their Revolution. Mao criticised Confucius' belief in the importance of a hierarchical social structure as particularly counter-revolutionary, even though he himself borrowed the Confucian concept of loyalty to one's ruler to garner popular support and further his own political goals. One important step that he took to challenge the traditional Confucian social hierarchy was to change the terms that the Chinese used to address each other, such as *jiejie* (meaning 'older sister' but also used for a slightly older woman) and *meimei* ('younger sister' or a younger woman), thus eliminating, or at least lessening, social inequality. Under Mao, everyone was to be addressed simply as *tongzhi*, or 'comrade'. Mao also banned texts such as *The Analects*, which contained Confucius' principal teachings, and Confucian scholars were punished and often tortured. Confucian temples were either turned into museums and libraries or were destroyed, and statues of Confucius inside them were defaced.

However, despite the demonisation of Confucius under Mao, the philosopher and his teachings have endured in the People's Republic of China and now, at the start of the twenty-first century, Confucius has again become an icon considered by many to be the source of much of their cultural heritage. Even under Mao, his influence was tangible, as Mao portrayed himself as the benevolent leader and the Chinese people generally showed him remarkable loyalty. Today, although Communism is still the official state ideology, certain Confucian values continue to be upheld, often in new, slightly modified ways. The government expects loyalty and respect from the people, and in return it is the role of the state to provide for, enrich and educate them – a concept that Communism and Confucianism share. Education is still highly valued, and scholars are generally well respected socially, though watched carefully by the authorities. The scholarly artistic pursuits of painting and calligraphy – which have long been important in China as a means of cultivating the spirit, expressing Confucian ideals and displaying cultural sophistication – are still highly revered and are the most respected art forms in China even today. Confucian temples are visited by many who wish to pay their respects to the Great Sage but also those hoping for academic success. The structure of the Chinese family has changed dramatically as a result of the Single Child Policy begun in 1979 by Deng Xiaoping, so one of the five basic relationships that Confucius emphasised – that of older and younger sibling – rarely exists in a whole generation, and the burden of caring for parents, the elderly and the deceased falls heavily on one child. Nonetheless, it is still expected.

It is worth noting here that the status of Confucianism in Taiwan over the last decades has been different. Under the Kuomintang, the Taiwanese government made a break from institutional Confucianism, in which the emperor oversaw an elaborate bureaucracy, which largely comprised scholar-gentlemen trained in the teachings of Confucianism.[18] However, because Taiwan regarded itself as the true custodian of Chinese culture as mainland Communists rejected their cultural past, it did not demonise Confucius and continued to revere him as an important cultural figure. Nor has the basic structure of family relationships changed there, so despite its dramatic political shifts over the past half-century or so, the presence of Confucianism in the lives of Taiwanese Chinese has been more openly acknowledged than on the mainland.

Confucianism in Korea

Korea is generally considered to be the most Confucian country in all of East Asia at present – even more so than mainland China, Taiwan or Japan.[19] Confucianism first entered the Korean peninsula along with Buddhism from China during the Three Kingdoms period (c. 57 BC–AD 668). From the late fourth century onwards, first in Koguryo (Goguryeo) in the north, then Paekche (Baekje) in the south-west, and finally Silla in the south-east, the governments of each kingdom promoted Confucian values as a means of maintaining and strengthening their aristocratic social orders. To this end, the kingdoms each established Confucian educational institutions and promoted the Chinese classics. Enthusiasm for both Buddhist and Confucian teachings was so great in Paekche that royal representatives from there took texts from both traditions to Japan to introduce them to the Japanese emperor. Silla was the last of the three kingdoms to receive Confucianism, and in particular it embraced the Confucian ideal of loyalty in order to bolster the authority of its rulers.[20]

In AD 668, when Silla united much of the region, although it turned to Tang China for cultural inspiration it chose as its official philosophy Buddhism, which was currently in ascendance in China, rather than the native Chinese philosophy. However, Confucianism increasingly came to rival Buddhism as an alternative system of thought, and in 682 a National Confucian College was founded which, from the mid-eighth century onwards, had a curriculum that consisted of *The Analects* and other Confucian texts. The establishment of this national educational institution led to the inauguration of the state examination system for the selection of government officials in 788, a system which stood in opposition to the traditional Silla aristocratic order. Towards the end of the Unified Silla period, Confucianism emerged as an ideology of political reform, with its proponents hoping to establish at its core a different kind of centralised aristocratic state staffed with men of talent who possessed a Confucian training.[21]

During the Koryo (Goryeo) period (918–1392), Buddhism continued to have a significant impact on the broader culture of Korea, but Confucianism grew in strength as an ideology of political reform. The fourth Koryo king, Kwangjong (Gwangjong) (949–75), and his grandson, the sixth Koryo king, Songjong (Seongjong) (960–97; r. 981–97), both attempted to strengthen the central government by adopting a Chinese-style imperial bureaucracy based on Confucian teachings and opening government positions up to more members of the hereditary aristocracy than had been possible under the Silla. They gave new life to the civil service examinations that had first been established under the Silla. Known in Korean as *kwago* (*gwageo*), these examinations tested students not only on their technical knowledge but also on their mastery of Chinese classics, including the teachings of Confucius. In 992 Songjong founded an academy, or National University, in the Koryo capital of Kaesong to provide advanced training in the Chinese classics. This academy, or *Gukjagam*, became the country's highest educational institution of the era and provided tuition for a higher number of young aristocrats than had previously been possible. Partly in an attempt to integrate the country aristocracy into the new bureaucratic system, Seongjong also established the twelve administrative divisions throughout the country, dispatched scholars to each of the local divisions to oversee local education, and brought local youths to study in the capital.[22]

It was under the Choson (Joseon) dynasty (1392–1910) that Confucianism had the most profound impact on Korean culture. Buddhism fell out of favour with the ruling elite and the Neo-Confucian philosophy of Song China, known in Korean as *songnihak* (*seongnihak*), was adopted as the official Choson ideology. The Confucianisation of the government administration that had begun centuries earlier was strengthened in the first century of Choson rule. The ruling class, or *yangban*, which comprised both the scholarly and military elite, were fully educated in Confucian ideals, and during this period the sons of the *yangban* class took the civil service examinations and attained prized government positions. At this time, Confucian beliefs and attitudes permeated nearly all areas of society, not only dictating how government was run and the type of education the country's young received, but also the ways in which people interacted socially. Social interaction at all levels was based on Confucian ideas and ideals such as *chung* (loyalty); *hyo* (filial piety); *in* (benevolence); and *sin* (trust). Confucian schools were built throughout the country equipped with a curriculum based on these principles. Their large libraries were stocked with Confucian texts both in Korean and Chinese, and classes were taught by foreign and local teachers trained in the Chinese classics. Korean literature of the period featured Confucian themes of loyalty and filial piety and much of the finest art was influenced by the literati themes of the *yangban* class and the restrained aesthetics associated with Confucian ideals of austerity and humility.

The Neo-Confucian ideals adopted by the Choson regime had a particularly profound impact on women. In early Korean history women had enjoyed many rights and freedoms. There were several Silla queens and women often exerted a powerful influence in the court. Although their status significantly diminished by the Koryo period, women still had property and inheritance entitlements and they were able to participate in rituals for the family ancestors. During the early Choson period, however, in an attempt to control the country's morality, the government issued regulations forcing women to remain secluded in their homes, and women of all classes were required to wear veils whenever they did leave home. Only close family members were allowed to see their faces. Women were required to be obedient and loyal towards the male members of their families – first their fathers, then their husbands, then their sons. In fact, their whole identity was based on their relationship to men, as they were not addressed by their own names; instead they were called 'wife of Younghi' or 'mother of Byung Hyo'. Their names were not recorded in their family registries, they had no inheritance rights and they were excluded from rituals in honour of the family ancestors. Although marriage offered women some social security, a man could divorce his wife for a number of 'evils', including loquaciousness and jealousy or for failing to bear a son. This oppression of women in the name of Confucian values continued until the early twentieth century, and remnants of it are still visible in modern Korea.[23]

During the sixteenth century Confucianism as a philosophy flourished in Korea, under the influence of two prominent Choson period philosophers, Yi Hwang (1501–70) and Yi I (1536–84), who offered markedly different interpretations of Neo-Confucian ideas. Yi Hwang, also known as T'oegye, closely followed the teachings of Zhu Xi and emphasised the importance of *li*, or moral principle (Korean: *i*), stressing that personal experience and ethical self-cultivation are the essence of learning. He departed from Zhu Xi in his explanation of *qi*, or matter (Korean: *ki*), which he considered were not inseparably related to one another; instead, he believed that *li* formed the basis of *qi*. His version of the Neo-Confucian doctrine not only gained a widespread following in Korea but impacted on Confucian thinkers in Japan. Yi I's approach to *li* and *qi* was the opposite of Yi Hwang's. He argued that the material, energising force of *qi* – and not the mysterious formative power of *li* – was the fundamental factor in the existence of the universe. His attitude to learning was more outward than inward, as he advocated external experience and breadth of learning over self-reflection and self-cultivation. Yi Hwang and Yi I are regarded as such philosophical giants in Korea that their faces both appear on the national currency.

In the late seventeenth century, some Korean Confucians began reacting to the metaphysical aspects of Neo-Confucianism and sought social reforms in a movement known as Sirhak (*Silhak*), or 'Practical Learning'. Followers of this movement, many of whom were *yangban* scholars who had been excluded from government office, opposed the formalism and ritual emphasised by Neo-Confucians and rejected its metaphysical nature, claiming that it was disconnected from the rapid agricultural, industrial and political changes occurring at the time. Openly critical of the current government, which they believed was not serving the people adequately, they advocated a more empirical Confucianism that was deeply concerned with human society at the practical level, and they attempted to reform the social structure and agricultural system and develop commerce and industry. To them, true learning was the acquisition of practical skills, and alongside the Chinese classics they encouraged the study of geography, agriculture and natural science. Their various reforms over the next century or so of the Choson period have been credited with helping to modernise Korean society.

The Confucian government administration system began to break down in the later nineteenth century, and by the early twentieth century the Choson dynasty had collapsed. Korea was annexed by Japan for almost forty years, thus losing its own government entirely. After 1945, when the peninsula was split into North and South Korea, both Koreas have been governed by systems that are a far cry from the earlier Chinese-style monarchy bolstered by a large and complex bureaucracy of scholarly officials educated in the Chinese Confucian classics. South Korea is a democracy, and although Confucianism no longer underlies the government or education system and much of the population considers itself to be non-religious, a substantial majority of South Koreans observe the basic

Confucian rituals, such as ancestral services and burial rites, and subscribe to Confucian values.[24] These values are not passed on through schools, church services or the mass media, but from within the family. Even in the Westernised structure of South Korean society today, more emphasis is placed on the group than on the individual, and great importance is given to such values as respect and loyalty towards elder family members, hard work and discipline, righteousness and sincerity. Education is also highly regarded, and as a result children experience considerable pressure to study hard in order to advance academically. In North Korea, which has been a Communist country, and thus socially very different from the South, since 1945, many of the same Confucian values exist – in particular loyalty to the country's leader and the emphasis on the group over the individual. Both Kim Il-Sung and Kim Jong-Il have adopted aspects of Confucius' teachings. They have promoted the idea that a ruler has exclusive rights to make decisions about his country, speak for the people, impose a strict hierarchical social order and demand absolute loyalty, while also fostering the concept of *juche*, or 'self-reliance', which teaches that the populace are not to rely on gods since human beings, in particular their leaders, are quite capable of making wise decisions.[25] However, it is doubtful that Confucius would have approved of the lack of concern that these two leaders have apparently shown for the well-being of North Koreans.

Confucianism in Japan

The earliest Japanese chronicles tell that Confucianism was introduced to Japan in AD 285, when a native of the Korean kingdom of Paekche brought copies of *The Analects* and other Confucian texts there. Although the date of this event may actually have been a century or so later, it is probable that the teachings of Confucius were known by some of the immigrants who reached Japan at this time.[26] These beliefs were very likely the Han dynasty form of Confucianism, which contained elements of Buddhist and Daoist philosophy, and not simply ethical teachings of Confucius and his followers. In the first centuries after its arrival in Japan the philosophy did not enjoy popular appeal, in part because it was eclipsed by Buddhism, which was gaining in force throughout East Asia at this time. Where it did have impact was in government institutions. Prince Shotoku (573–621), who served as regent to Empress Suiko (524–628) during the Asuka period (538–710, or 552–710), was instrumental in establishing Japan's early centralised government, modelled largely on that of Sui (581–618) and Tang dynasty (618–906) China. Shotoku adopted Chinese legal and bureaucratic institutions, establishing a hierarchical bureaucracy with twelve official court ranks, and outlining in AD 604 the basic principles of government in the *Seventeen Article Constitution*. The first article reads: 'Harmony is to be valued, and an avoidance of wanton opposition to be honoured. All men are influenced by partisanship, and there are few who are intelligent. Hence there are some who disobey their lords and fathers, or who maintain feuds with neighbouring villages. But when those above are harmonious and those below are friendly, and there is concord in the discussion of business, right views of things spontaneously gain acceptance. Then what is there which cannot be accomplished?'[27] This article, which maintains that harmonious relationships are the key to successful government, is drawn straight from Confucius' teachings and shows the importance given to his philosophy by Shotoku. Later articles recommend certain Buddhist doctrines as a means of achieving this harmony. This concept of a Confucian social and government order supported by Buddhist practice and the insights of Buddhist psychology was the philosophy of government that remained dominant in Japan for at least a millennium.[28]

Shotoku also looked to Confucianism as a way of strengthening imperial power. While he undoubtedly had the well-being of the Japanese people in mind, his ultimate goal as regent was to establish a powerful centralised government and reinforce the Emperor's claims to being the Son of Heaven. Although it is often thought that the concept of Japanese imperial rule is based simply on the assertion of unbroken succession from the Sun Goddess, the idea of the absolute power of the emperor, or Tenno ('Divine ruler'), also reflects the Chinese concept of the sovereign as the possessor of the Mandate of Heaven, an important aspect of Confucian teachings.[29]

From around the eighth century onwards Buddhism gained remarkable momentum in Japan, and over the following centuries, beginning with the ruling classes, various forms of Buddhism spread widely throughout the population, dwarfing the impact of the other imported philosophies of Confucianism and Daoism. During this time, while both Confucian and Daoist ideas continued to be circulated among Japan's philosophers, scholars and literary figures, the presence of Confucianism was limited mainly to the bureaucratic, social and ethical structures of Japanese society. In the early thirteenth century the Neo-Confucianist teachings of Zhu Xi were introduced to Japan, but because they were originally transmitted there by Zen Buddhist monks they were largely studied within the context of Zen Buddhism, the dominant form of Buddhism practised by Japan's military rulers and their retainers. For nearly four centuries Neo-Confucianism (*Shushigaku*) was regarded by Zen Buddhists as a stimulating mental exercise that, if used properly, might point towards the same truths as Zen.[30] That Neo-Confucianism was only practised within Zen Buddhism is somewhat ironic, since Zhu Xi had originally developed his teachings in part as a rational alternative to Buddhist philosophy.

In the early seventeenth century, after a presence of 1,000 years in Japan, the teachings of Confucius – primarily the Neo-Confucian version – gained the support of the Tokugawa government, which was looking for an ideology that could help them maintain social order after decades of civil war.[31] As Japan's new rulers, the Tokugawa eagerly touted the concept of the Heavenly Mandate, claiming that they were the new recipients of this mandate. They also adopted Neo-Confucianist concepts of social hierarchy, in which Zhu Xi expanded on Confucius' belief in the importance of behaving according to one's social position by linking this order to a universal order. Zhu Xi claimed that, just as there is a larger universal Way, there is a Way of the ruler, a Way of the parent, a Way of the child and so on.[32] Based on this concept, the Tokugawa enforced a rigid social structure known as *shi-no-ko-sho*, which placed the samurai (*shi*) at the top of society, followed by farmers (*no*), artisans (*ko*) and merchants (*sho*) at the bottom, and tightly controlled it for over 250 years. Confucius' teachings permeated all these levels of society. The samurai, who were no longer called on to fight in battle, were now trained as bureaucrats and the Confucian classics formed a significant part of their education. Many samurai even became Confucian scholars and opened private schools all around Japan. The government also increasingly provided education for the lower classes, and the curriculum contained many of the moralistic, ethical aspects of Confucius' teachings, such as filial piety, honouring family ancestors and loyalty to the shogun, or military leader. Interestingly, while Confucius emphasised loyalty to one's parents over loyalty to one's lord, the influence of samurai ethics, or *bushido* (the 'Way of the warrior), which stressed devotion to one's lord over all else, created a point of conflict in Japanese culture.

Although Neo-Confucianism undoubtedly greatly impacted on Tokugawa Japan, it is worth noting that, within government and intellectual circles, there was considerable debate over how to adapt Confucian teachings to Japanese concerns. For some scholars, such as Hayashi Razan (1583–1687), the teachings of Zhu Xi were the most effective way to order Japanese society, while later scholars such as Ogyu Sorai (1666–1728), who very likely considered himself a sage transmitting the Way of Confucius and other early philosophers,[33] proposed a return to the ancient Confucian texts in an attempt to access the true teachings of Confucius. Others still, like Motoori Norinaga (1730–1801), sought the wisdom of the ancients, but not the Chinese ancients. Rather, he advocated a study of the ancient texts of Japan, and created a nativist philosophical movement that owed much structurally to Confucian thought. These conflicting approaches towards Confucianism continued throughout the period, with the nativist approach gaining increasing support in the nineteenth century. In 1868 the Tokugawa military government was overthrown and political power was returned to the Emperor. Many of the Chinese cultural associations of the Tokugawa military leaders were shed in an attempt to bolster Japanese imperial power and absorb Western culture, and Confucianism lost its position as an official ideology.

In modern Japan, despite the nationalistic ideology that prevailed in the first half of the twentieth century and the large-scale Westernisation of much of Japanese culture over the course of the century, the influence of Confucius' teachings can still be seen clearly. The Japanese famously regard the welfare of the group as more important than that of the individual, and loyalty to one's family, company, teachers and government continues to be deeply valued.

A good education is considered to be of the utmost importance, and school examinations effectively rule children's lives until they reach university. Showing respect for one's parents, parents-in-law, elders and ancestors continues to be stressed and plays a major part in social rituals and festivals. Homes typically contain a small family altar to which food, drink and incense are regularly offered, and festivals such as O-bon, held in the later summer, welcome ancestor spirits back home and graves are swept in their honour. The Japanese are also well known as a society for their exceptional politeness towards others, a quality that can also surely be attributed in part to their absorption of Confucius' teachings.

Confucianism in Vietnam

Confucianism has also been a powerful cultural and social force in Vietnam. In 111 BC an area that is now the north of Vietnam and which the Chinese called Nanyue, or 'Southern Yue', was annexed by Han dynasty China. For the next 900 years or so the region was ruled intermittently by China and absorbed much of Chinese culture. For centuries, the everyday attitudes and behaviour of the Vietnamese people were dictated by a synthesis of religions and philosophies, including Buddhism, Daoism and Confucianism, which came into the peninsula from China, as well as their own native beliefs in honouring ancestors and heroic figures. Although, for much of their history, the Vietnamese have considered themselves primarily Buddhist, Confucianism also began to leave its mark on Vietnamese society in the early years AD. The Chinese regime in Nanyue was initially lenient but a revolt in the first century AD prompted China to tighten its control of Vietnam, by establishing a Chinese-style administrative system of prefectures and districts ruled by scholar-officials sent by the Han government. Chinese administrators replaced most former local officials, but some members of the Vietnamese aristocracy were allowed to fill lower positions in the bureaucracy. These aristocrats were thoroughly educated in Chinese language and cultural, religious and political traditions. Confucian values were promoted: loyalty to the ruler, filial piety and self-betterment through education were of particular importance. Under the Tang dynasty (618–906), civil service examinations were established for children of the upper classes, and Confucian texts formed the basis of the curriculum. Despite the creation of a solid Confucian bureaucratic, family and social structure in the region, many native traditions were retained at all levels of society, and the attempt to sinicise Vietnam had the effect both of drawing the Vietnamese closer to China culturally, while also instilling in them resistance and hostility towards their Chinese overlords.[34]

When the Vietnamese achieved independence from China in AD 939 they retained many Chinese cultural traditions, including a devotion to Confucian social values. The Ly dynasty (1010–1225) established its own bureaucratic government structure and Confucian-based civil service examinations formulated on Chinese models. In 1070 the Confucian Temple of Literature, or Van Mieu, was established in Hanoi, and within a few years it became the site of an imperial academy, the country's first university, where bureaucrats, royalty and members of the upper classes received a Confucian-style education for over 700 years. In 1407 Vietnam was again conquered by China. Ming China ruled Vietnam as if it were a Chinese province, attempting to stamp out Buddhism at court and forcing the Vietnamese government to adopt Ming-style Neo-Confucianism. Although Ming rule was brief, its impact was again profound, as Vietnamese rulers and thinkers continued to look to

Ming China as a source of political and cultural ideas. The following Le dynasty (1428–1788), which reclaimed Vietnamese independence, chose again to adopt a Chinese-style centralised government, bureaucracy and educational system. One of the most celebrated Le rulers, Le Thanh Tong (c. 1460–97), was a great proponent of Confucian studies and continued to encourage them as the foundation of the Le dynasty civil service examinations. However, he also ordered the formulation of a legal code that recognised the higher position of women in Vietnamese society than in Chinese society, or other cultures influenced by China. Under the new code, parental consent was not required for marriage, and daughters were granted equal inheritance rights with sons.[35]

From the fifteenth century onwards, Confucian values were promoted widely within the education system as schools were opened nationwide, offering Confucian-based elementary education in small villages. Much Vietnamese literature of this period was also coloured with Confucian ideals, and musical performances containing Confucian themes were held throughout the country, to help bring Confucian principles to the illiterate sections of the population. In particular, the Vietnamese opera or Hat Boi (also known as Tuong in the north), which was modelled on Chinese opera, was performed to audiences from the aristocracy to the peasantry and touched on important themes such as benevolence, filial piety and loyalty.

During the following centuries of Vietnam's history, Confucianism continued to be a powerful force in government and education until the French colonisation from 1887 to 1954, when the traditional Confucian-based education system was dismantled and replaced by a European model. However, Confucian values continued to play a significant role in daily life and family structures, even during the ensuing Vietnam War and current Communist rule, although many Vietnamese fled Vietnam rather than live under a Communist regime. The Vietnamese, both in Vietnam and over-seas, continue to practise Buddhism or Christianity; yet a strong Confucian respect for education, intense loyalty and piety towards parents, and the rituals honouring family ancestors all colour Viet-namese culture to this day.

Other areas in South-east Asia

It is important to note here that other countries in South-east Asia have also been influenced by Confucian beliefs, even though their governments did not adopt the Confucian-based bureaucratic and education systems of China. Over the centuries, large numbers of ethnic Chinese have been driven by economic and political factors to migrate to areas of South-east Asia. The first major wave of immigration was spurred by trading activities in the early fifteenth century, a second wave during the Opium Wars in the nineteenth century, and a third around the first half of the twentieth century, when China underwent considerable political unrest. Chinese migrants settled in Malaysia, Singapore, Indonesia, the Philippines, Burma (Myanmar), Cambodia and Laos, often becoming involved in commerce. These overseas Chinese espouse several different reli-gious traditions, including Buddhism, Islam and Christianity, but they also follow many of the ethical teachings of Confucius, and consider him to have been a great and moral teacher.

Confucianism in the West

In the seventeenth century, when Portuguese Jesuit missionaries first entered China, their goal was to convert as many Chinese as possible to Christianity. They made a great effort to study and understand the existing Chinese religious and philosophical systems so that they could better understand the Chinese and find the most effective means of converting them. They regarded Buddhism and Daoism as rival religions that were incompatible with Christian thought, but were fascinated by Confucius, whom they considered to be a prince of philosophers. They believed that his teachings were consistent with Christianity since Confucius focused on the effort of the individual to behave virtuously, and did not speak of worship of a particular god – in fact, they believed that Confucius' god was the same as theirs. In a move that sparked a major controversy within the Church, they argued that Chinese Catholics should be allowed to continue practising certain Confucian rites, in particular the ceremonies honouring their ancestors. Determined to convince the Vatican of the secular nature of Confucius' teachings and the importance of allowing Chinese Christians to continue to follow them, the Jesuits translated Confucian texts into European languages. One such text was the *Confucius Sinarum Philosophus*, a compendium of the *Four Books* of Confucianism published in France in 1687. These texts were disseminated widely in Europe, but they failed to convince the central Christian authority. Because Confucianism was so popular among the Chinese people, Pope Clement XI considered it a threat to the spread of Christianity in China, and in 1715 he forbade Chinese Catholics to perform ancestral rites.

However, the efforts of the Jesuits to defend Confucius and his teachings had an unexpected impact in Europe. His doctrines caught the attention of many European philosophers and other intellectuals who were engaged in the critical questioning of traditional institutions, customs and morals, in particular those imposed by theocracies and aristocracies. During the so-called Age of Reason of the late seventeenth century and the Age of Enlightenment, which peaked in the eighteenth, a number of significant European philosophers embraced Confucius as a great sage whose emphasis on the individual cultivation of virtue and insistence that kings should also cultivate such integrity echoed many of their own theories. For example, the German thinker Gottfried Leibniz (1646–1716) referred to Confucius as 'the king of Chinese philosophers', and argued that Europeans had much to learn from Chinese morality.[36] In France, the writer and philosopher Voltaire (1694–1778) upheld Confucius as a great rationalist, who 'appeals only to virtue, he preaches no miracles, there is nothing in [his books] of religious allegory'.[37] He believed that an enlightened ruler could learn from the teachings of Confucius and, as if following in Confucius' own footsteps, he wrote to King Frederick the Great of Prussia, in the hope that the monarch would hire him as an adviser. As had happened to Confucius many centuries before, the monarch turned Voltaire down.

Over the following centuries, European philosophers and intellectuals continued to study Confucius and acknowledge his significance as a major world philosopher, and his teachings undoubtedly influenced the works of many European and other thinkers and writers. In the nineteenth century, Westerners, in particular the British, travelled increasingly to China and some of them made important studies of Confucius' teachings. The noted Scottish Sinologist James Legge (1815–97) went to China as a missionary and remained there for thirty years, learning the language and making numerous translations of Chinese texts, including the principal Confucian texts, to which he added his own commentaries. Works such as his have made the teachings of Confucius more widely available to the English-speaking world. Throughout the twentieth century, increasing numbers of Chinese immigrated to Europe, the Americas and Australia, taking with them many of their traditional values, such as the importance of education and respect for parents and ancestors. The presence of overseas Chinese and other East Asians in local communities worldwide, coupled with China's growing economic, political and cultural presence on the world stage, has sparked an enormous interest in Chinese culture, and at the core of any study of China – in a book, at a school, university, or at one of the Chinese government-sponsored Confucius Institutes – is an introduction to the country's most celebrated teacher and philosopher.

Now, in the early twenty-first century, the name of Confucius is widely recognised in most cultures even though his teachings may not yet be well understood by the average American, Australian, African or European. Regrettably, many people associate him with the nuggets of wisdom that are often found on fortune cookies in Chinese restaurants, or with silly jokes like 'Confucius say, "Man with only one chopstick go hungry."'[38] And recently I was directed to a CNN clip of the Miss Panama 2009 contest, where one hopeful was asked to explain who Confucius was and replied, 'Confucius was one of whom invented confusion. And that's why ... ehhh. One of the most ancient he was one of the Chinese ... Japanese who was most ancient. Thank you.'[39] At least she had a feeling that he was Chinese and lived a long time ago, but how heart-breaking for Confucius that she blamed him for the invention of confusion, when his life's work was focused on bringing order to a chaotic, confused world!

Despite the occasional confusion about who Confucius was and the fogginess regarding the details of his life, it seems quite clear, twenty-six centuries after he lived and died, that he did realise his goal of making a name for himself. He could not have imagined how widely known his name would become, nor how long his teachings would be studied, debated and practised at all levels of society. Having had so little success convincing rulers of his own time to adopt his theories, he would probably have laughed at the suggestion that not only the government of his own country but also those of neighbouring nations would eventually base many of their policies on his teachings. Although Confucius struggled with poverty, lack of employment, homelessness and a sense of failure for much of his life, his dedication to his Way was indeed worthwhile and has enriched the lives of many millions of people throughout history. His ideals of ethical integrity in human relations, kindness and respect at all levels of society and self-cultivation through education have endured longer than any imperial dynasty and have become an important contribution to the world's treasury of wisdom.

Notes

Preface

1   Chin, Annping, *The Authentic Confucius: A Life of Thought and Politics* (New York: Scribner, 2007), p. 3.

2   I chose to use Simon Leys' version of *The Analects* (New York/London, W.W. Norton, 1997) for this biography because his text used the *pinyin* rather than Wade-Giles transliteration of Chinese words and names, which is consistent with the rest of my text. I also felt that his translation is slightly easier for a modern reader to follow. However, I must point out that I had problems with some of his commentaries, particularly his own anti-homosexual views, which I believe have no place in a translation. Two more respected translations of *The Analects* are those by Arthur Waley and D.C. Lau, which are included in the bibliography.

Introduction: China's Great Sage

1   Leys, *The Analects*, 5.13, p. 21.

2   Leys, *The Analects*, 6.22, p. 27.

3   Although Confucius is often credited with inventing the term *ren*, it existed before his time but was not used widely and may have

simply referred to the kindness shown by a lord to his subject. As a key concept in the teachings of Confucius, it gained wider usage.

4   Leys, *The Analects*, 9.1, p. 39.

5   Leys, *The Analects*, 6.22, p. 27. Note that Arthur Waley translates this obscure phrase differently, as 'Goodness cannot be obtained until what is difficult has been duly done.' Waley, *The Analects of Confucius* (New York: Random House, Vintage Books, 1989), Chapter 6.20, p. 120.

6   Leys, *The Analects*, 7.30, p. 32.

7   Leys, *The Analects*, 4.6, pp. 15–16.

8   Leys, *The Analects*, 7.16, p. 31.

9   Leys, *The Analects*, 4.2, p. 15.

10   Leys, *The Analects*, 4.2, p. 15.

11   Leys, *The Analects*, 4.5, p. 15.

12   For an enlightening discussion of this seeming contradiction, see Chapter 3 of Fingarette, Herbert, *Confucius: The Secular as Sacred* (Prospect Heights, Illinois: Waveland Press, Inc.), 1972.

13   Leys, *The Analects*, 8.7, p. 36.

14   Leys, *The Analects*, 15.8, p. 75.

15   Leys, *The Analects*, 8.2, p. 35.

16   Leys, *The Analects*, 2.8, p. 7.

17   Leys, *The Analects*, 2.7, p. 7.

18   Leys, *The Analects*, 3.4, p. 10.

19   Leys, *The Analects*, 3.12, p. 12.

20   Leys, *The Analects*, 3.3, p. 10.

21   Leys, *The Analects*, 16.9, pp. 82–83.

22   Leys, *The Analects*, 9.19, p. 41.

23   Leys, *The Analects*, 14.24, p. 70.

24   Leys, *The Analects*, 7.8, p. 30.

25   Leys, *The Analects*, 12.15, p. 58.

26   Leys, *The Analects*, 15.22, p. 77.

27   Leys, *The Analects*, 15.36, p. 78.

28   Leys, *The Analects*, 12.4, p. 56.

29   Leys, *The Analects*, 15.18, p. 76.

30   Leys, *The Analects*, 4.5, p. 15.

31   Leys, *The Analects*, 15.32, p. 78.

32   Leys, *The Analects*, 6.30, p. 28.

33   Leys, *The Analects*, 14.23, p. 70.

34   Leys, *The Analects*, 15.21, p. 77.

35   Leys, *The Analects*, 4.16, p. 17.

36   Leys, *The Analects*, 2.14, p. 7.

37   Leys, *The Analects*, 17.24, p. 89.

38   Leys, *The Analects*, 16.8, p. 82.

39   Leys, *The Analects*, 16.7, p. 82.

40   Leys, *The Analects*, 14.22, p. 70.

41   Leys, *The Analects*, 18.6, p. 91.

42   Leys, *The Analects*, 18.7, p. 92.

43   Leys, *The Analects*, 1.6, p. 4.

44   Leys, *The Analects*, 1.2, p. 3.

45   Leys, *The Analects*, 15.24, p. 77.

46   Leys, *The Analects*, 2.19, p. 8.

47   Leys, *The Analects*, 13.2, p. 60.

48   Leys, *The Analects*, 1.5, p. 4.

49   Leys, *The Analects*, 13.16, p. 63.

50   Leys, *The Analects*, 4.13, p. 16.

51   Leys, *The Analects*, 12.2, p. 55.

52   Leys, *The Analects*, 5.16, p. 21.

53   Leys, *The Analects*, 12.19, p. 58.

54   Leys, *The Analects*, 2.20, p. 8.

55   Leys, *The Analects*, 12.2, p. 55.

56   Leys, *The Analects*, 2.3, p. 6.

57   Leys, *The Analects*, 12.7, p. 56.

58   Leys, *The Analects*, 2.1, p. 6.

59   Leys, *The Analects*, 1.1, p. 3.

60   Leys, *The Analects*, 7.19, p. 31.

Chapter 1: The Bitter Gourd That Is Not Eaten

1   This lament was recorded by Han dynasty historian Sima Qian in his biography of Confucius. See Yang Hsien-yi and Gladys Yang (translators and editors), *Selections from Records of the Historian by Szuma Chien* (Beijing: Foreign Languages Press, 1979), p. 13. It is also included in *The Analects* as 'Am I a bitter gourd, only to hang as decoration, but unfit to be eaten?' See Leys, *The Analects*, Chapter 17.7, p. 85.

2   The version of the incident described in this chapter has drawn on Pierre Do-Dinh's description. See Do-Dinh, Pierre (translated by Charles Lam Markmann), *Confucius and Chinese Humanism* (New York: Funk & Wagnalls, 1969), pp. 76–8. Sima Qian recounts this incident in Chen province and the exchange between Confucius and his disciples in some detail. See Yang and Yang, *Records of the Historian*, pp. 17–19. A much shorter version of the exchange between Confucius and Zilu is also found in *The Analects*. See Leys, *The Analects*, 15.2, p. 74.

Chapter 2: China at the Time of Confucius

1   Although Confucius apparently did not discuss the concept of Heaven in his teachings and had little interest in the supernatural or mystical, he did allude to what he believed to be his Heavenly mission on several occasions. In *The Analects*, for example, he made such claims as, 'At fifty, I knew the will of Heaven' (see Leys, *The Analects*, 2.4, p. 6) and 'Heaven vested me with moral power' (*The Analects*, 7.23, p. 32). He also lamented, 'No one understands me! ... If I am understood, it must be by Heaven' (*The Analects*, 14.35, p. 71) and called upon Heaven to punish him if he had erred: 'If I have done wrong, may Heaven confound me! May Heaven confound me!' (*The Analects*, 6.28, p. 27).

2   For an illuminating discussion of the Axial Age, see Karen

Armstrong's *The Great Transformation: The Beginning of Our Religious Traditions* (New York: Anchor Books, 2006).

3   The *Shujing* and many other texts were written by historians employed by the Zhou court, so their accounts of history tend to be biased in favour of the Zhou rulers.

4   Faulkenhausen, Lothar von, *Chinese Society in the Age of Confucius: The Archaeological Evidence* (Los Angeles: Cotsen Institute of Archaeology UCLA, 2006), Chapters 1 and 2.

5   Ebrey, Patricia Buckley, *The Cambridge Illustrated Encyclopedia of China* (Cambridge: Cambridge University Press, 1999), p. 39.

6   Leys, *The Analects*, 16.2, p. 81.

Chapter 3: Early Life and Family

1   Confucius' father's name Shuliang He is a combination of his 'style' name or *zi*, Shuliang, and his personal name or *ming*, He. It would be more typical to refer to him by a combination of his clan name, Kong, and his personal name, Shuliang, so Kong Shuliang, just as Confucius was known as Kong Zhongni as an adult. It is not clear why his name is recorded in this manner (e-mail correspondence with Jonathan Markley, February, 2009).

2   For more on ancient Chinese beliefs about the afterlife and ancestors, see Dien, Albert, 'Chinese Beliefs in the Afterworld', in *The Quest for Eternity: Chinese Ceramic Sculptures from the People's Republic of China* (Los Angeles San Francisco: the Los Angeles County Museum of Art/Chronicle Books, 1987), pp. 1–15.

3   Confucius' ancestry is outlined in Clements, Jonathan, *Confucius: A Biography* (Stroud: Sutton Publishing, 2004), pp. 3–6, and in Legge, James, *Confucius: Confucian Analects, The Great Learning & The Doctrine of the Mean* (Clarendon Press, Oxford, 1893–5. Reprint, Mineola: New York: Dover edition 1971), pp. 56–8.

4   This issue of whether or not Confucius' parents were married has caused much debate among scholars, mainly because of the Chi-

nese phrase *yehe*, used by Sima Qian in his biography to describe their union. Jonathan Clements notes that the phrase *yehe* can mean 'torrid' and 'common-law', which has led many scholars to believe that their union was illegitimate, and that Zhengzai never became his wife. He suggests, however, that the idea of 'wild' in this context is more likely to refer to the disparity in their ages, which was not typical at the time. See Clements, Jonathan, *Confucius: A Biography*, p. 9 and notes p. 121.

Annping Chin translates the phrase *yehe* as 'he and the girl made love in the field'. Chin also proposes that Shuliang may have ended his first marriage because that wife failed to give him sons, and driven away the concubine who had borne him his disabled son, so they must have had a legitimate marriage. But then, she wonders, why did they make love in the fields? See Chin, Annping, *The Authentic Confucius: A Life of Thought and Politics* (New York: Scribner, 2007), pp. 24–5.

Some translations of Sima Qian, such as Yang and Yang, have avoided this issue by not translating the phrase *yehe* and simply stating, 'Shu-liang-heh took a daughter of the Yen family'. See Yang and Yang, *Records of the Historian*, p. 1.

5   Some scholars state that the disabled son, Mang-pi, was borne by a concubine, not the first wife. See Legge, *Confucius*, pp. 56–8. See also Chin, *The Authentic Confucius*, p. 24.

6   In traditional Chinese astrology, the five planets are Venus, Jupiter, Mercury, Mars and Saturn, corresponding to the Daoist Five Elements of metal, wood, water, fire and earth, respectively. The planets, and also many of the stars, were often regarded as spirits or deities and were believed to influence earthly events, especially the life and death of human beings. The appearance of the spirits of the five planets together would have been considered particularly auspicious.

7   See Legge, *Confucius*, p. 59, note 1.

8   This date is not definite. Sima Qian's account claims 551 BC, while sources, including Zhu Xi (1130–1200), the most important neo-

Confucianist thinker of the Song dynasty, claim he was born in the twenty-first year of Duke Xiang's reign, so 552 BC. The actual day of his birth is believed to have been the twentieth day of the tenth month of that year, but his birthday is now generally celebrated on 28 September of our solar calendar.

9   See Legge, *Confucius*, p. 59, note 1.

10   Yang and Yang, *Records of the Historian*, p. 1.

11   Clements, *Confucius*, p. 10.

12   Yang and Yang, *Records of the Historian*, p. 1.

13   Throughout his life, Confucius emphasised the importance of music in ritual, even correlating harmony in ceremonial music with a harmonious society. He suggested that good government is only possible if musical notes are harmonised; if the notes are out of order, chaos ensues. Music, therefore, was not merely for entertainment; it had a critical social and ritual function and must be performed correctly. This belief is reflected in his exclamation: 'They speak of music here, and music there – as if music merely meant bells and drums.' Leys, *The Analects*, 17.11, p. 87.

14   This verse is Song 20 from *The Book of Songs*, a collection of traditional songs and hymns that was likely compiled after Confucius' lifetime. This translation is taken from Waley, Arthur (translator), *The Book of Songs: The Ancient Chinese Classic of Poetry* (New York: Grove Press, 1996), p. 18.

15   Leys, *The Analects*, 17.9, p. 87.

16   See Note 13.

17   Yang and Yang, *Records of the Historian*, pp. 21–2.

18   Legge, *Confucius*, p. 60.

19   Leys, *The Analects*, 9.6, p. 40.

20   Leys, *The Analects*, 2.4, p. 6.

21   *Shu Jing (Shu Ching)*, translation by James Legge, reprinted by Hong Kong University Press, 1960, vol. III, p. 52, reproduced on http://www.chinapage.com/confucius/shujing-e.html. (Note: the names have been changed to Pinyin here.)

22   Clements, *Confucius*, pp. 12–13. Clements notes that some

sources report that the couple eventually divorced in their forties, but does not cite the sources.

23   The subject of Confucius' possible divorce is discussed further in Chapter 5.

24   See Legge, *Confucius*, p. 60. Sima Qian mentions his son's two names but does not explain their origin. See Yang and Yang, *Records of the Historian*, p. 26.

25   Leys, *The Analects*, 16.13, pp. 83–4.

26   The reaction of Confucius to the death of Yan Hui is discussed in *Lunyu* 11.8 to 11.11, translation by Simon Leys, p. 50.

27   Leys, *The Analects*, 5.1, p. 19.

28   Leys, *The Analects*, 17.25, p. 89.

29   There is little room here for a discussion on Confucianism, sexism and feminism. For a lively treatment of this topic, see Li, Chenyang (ed.), *The Sage and the Second Sex: Confucianism, Ethics, and Gender* (Chicago and La Salle, Illinois: Open Court, a division of Carus, 2000).

30   Mark Edward Lewis notes that despite their weak role in ancient Chinese society, women wielded considerable power in the home. 'The major basis of such power was the authority of the mother over her sons. In early imperial China, the authority of age took precedence over that of gender, and filial obedience to both male and female parents was a son's highest obligation.' See Lewis, Mark Edward, *The Construction of Space in Early China* (Albany: State University of New York Press, 2006), p. 106.

31   Leys, *The Analects*, 1.2, p. 3.

32   Leys, *The Analects*, 17.21, p. 89.

33   According to Sima Qian, his mother had hidden the location of his father's grave from Confucius, but after her death a woman from the village of Tsu revealed it to him and he buried her at Mount Fang with his father. Yang and Yang, *Records of the Historian*, p. 1.

34   This story is recounted both in Clements, *Confucius*, p. 18, and in Legge, *Confucius*, p. 62.

35   In the *Doctrine of the Mean* (*Zhongyong*), one of the Four Books
     (*Sishu*) selected in the Song dynasty (960–1279) to introduce the
     teachings of Confucius, Confucius is said to have lamented that
     he himself felt that he had failed in his roles as son, subject,
     younger brother and friend. If this is the case, his admiration for
     his mother's accomplishments would make perfect sense. How-
     ever, we should note that, like *The Analects*, this work was sup-
     posedly written by his grandson, Zisi, and so cannot be taken as
     his actual words. See Goldin, Paul Rakita, *The Culture of Sex in
     Ancient China* (Honolulu: University of Hawai'i Press, 2002),
     Chapter 3: 'Women and Sex Roles', p. 55.

Chapter 4: Early Career and Teachings

1   Sima Qian says that he managed the granaries of the Ji clan (the
    Jisun family), who were one of the three powerful families of the
    state of Lu – see Yang and Yang, *Records of the Historian*, p. 2.
2   Legge, *Confucius*, p. 60, quoting from Mencius, V. Pt. II v. 4.
3   Legge, *Confucius*, p. 61, quoting from Mencius, V. Pt. II v. 4.
4   Leys, *The Analects*, 2.11, p. 7.
5   Leys, *The Analects*, 7.1, p.29. Although, according to *The Analects*,
    Confucius claimed to have invented nothing, this has often been
    questioned. For example, some, including nineteenth-century
    Chinese scholar and political thinker Kang Youwei, have argued
    that he actually invented the 'golden age' of the Western Zhou
    dynasty to push his reform agenda. See Immanuel C.Y. Hsü, *The
    Rise of Modern China* (6th edition, Oxford University Press, 2000),
    p. 364.
6   Leys, *The Analects*, 2.2, p. 6.
7   Leys, *The Analects*, 13.5, p. 61.
8   Leys, *The Analects*, 2.15, p. 8.
9   Leys, *The Analects*, 7.8, p. 30.
10 Waley, Arthur (translator), *The Analects of Confucius* (New York:

Vintage Books, 1989) 7.7, p. 124. The Chinese word *shuxiu*
literally means 'a [small] bundle of [ten slices] of dried meat'.
Waley notes that one commentator translated the word to mean
'attained manhood', that is, the age of fourteen. However, the term
is generally accepted to mean 'dried meat', and is still used today
to refer to 'tuition fees'.

11 Although Confucius generally directed his teaching to males, the
character *ren* in the word *xiaoren* does not just mean 'man'. In
fact, it is more correctly translated as 'person', so *xiaoren* can
apply to petty-minded people of both sexes.

12 Leys, *The Analects*, 14.28, p. 70.

13 During the Eastern Zhou period, a limited education was
available to women of the upper classes. They were generally
taught within the confines of their homes by their own mothers
or mothers-in-law, and much of their study related to their roles
as mothers, wives and daughters-in-law. However, contemporary
texts tell of certain noblewomen who were knowledgeable in
rituals, morality and politics, and some of these women even
advised the male members of their family. Most famous is Lady
Jing, the mother of Gongfu Wenbo, an eminent Lu statesman
and contemporary of Confucius. According to the *Discourses of
the States (Guoyu)*, a collection of speeches and narratives from
the Eastern Zhou period, Lady Jing discussed politics and
morality with Gongfu Wenbo, blaming the desperate political
state of Lu on the fact that its rulers were uninformed and
indolent. She was also the great aunt of Ji Kangzi, the head of
the Jisun clan, and advised him that the key to a noble man's
posterity is hard work. She was an expert in ritual and was
praised for this knowledge and for her superior morality by
Confucius. According to Paul R. Gordon, the contemporary
stories about Lady Jing 'embody the belief that all men,
including those at the very apex of society, can learn from wise
women'. See Wang, Robin R. (ed.), *Images of Women in Chinese
Thought and Culture: Writings from the Pre-Qin Period through*

the Song Dynasty (Indianapolis: Hackett Publishing Co. Inc., 2003), Chapter 9, pp. 83–91.

14   Legge, *Confucius*, p. 115.

15   Legge, *Confucius*, p. 87.

16   Legge, *Confucius*, pp. 61–2, from *Liji*, II, Section 1.i.10; Section 2.iii.30, Muller (ed.)/Legge (trans.), *Sacred Books of China* (Oxford: Clarendon Press, 1885), vol. III, p. 369. See also Clements, *Confucius*, p. 18.

17   This episode is recounted in the *Zuo Zhuan* commentary of *The Spring and Autumn Annals*, under the seventh year of Duke Zhao of Lu. Legge, *Confucius*, pp. 62–3. It is likely that this encounter between Confucius and the Viscount of Tan, or at least the content of their discussion, was a later invention datable to the Warring States period, since the philosophical theories that they are said to have discussed were not formed in the time of Confucius (Conversation with Jonathan Markley, March 2009).

18   Waley, *The Analects*, 3.23, p. 100.

19   Clements, *Confucius*, p. 19.

20   Waley, *The Analects*, 2.4, p. 88.

21   This excerpt is taken from Legge, *Confucius*, pp. 63–4, quoting from the *Zuo Zhuan* commentary of *The Spring and Autumn Annals*, Duke Zhao, seventh year. Sima Qian recounts the same story but says that Meng Xizi died when Confucius was seventeen and his son joined Confucius as a disciple shortly afterwards (see Yang and Yang, *Records of the Historian*, pp. 1–2). In most later biographies, Confucius is said to have only started taking students in his twenties, making this chronology seem unlikely.

22   Yang and Yang, *Records of the Historian*, p. 2.

23   Leys, *The Analects*, 9.17, p. 41.

24   Sima Qian gives no details of the trip to Luoyang, stating simply, 'They went to Chou [the capital of Zhou] to study rites and there met Lao Tzu [Laozi].' The details here are drawn from Legge, *Confucius*, p. 66, who quotes from vol. II of *Narratives of the School (Jiayu)*, a Wei dynasty text (386–535) supposedly based on

an earlier text about Confucius. The edition used by Legge was edited by Li Yung in 1780 (see Legge's notes, p. 132).

25 Legge, *Confucius*, p. 66, quoting from the *Narratives of the School*, vol. II.

26 Yang and Yang, *Records of the Historian*, pp. 2–3.

27 Legge, *Confucius*, p. 65, quoting from Sima Qian's *Shiji*, Chapter 63. For translation see Nienhauser, William H., Jr. (editor), Tsai-fa Cheng, Zhongli Lu, William H. Nienhauser, Jr. and Robert Reynolds (translators), *The Grand Scribe's Records*, vol. 7, *Memoirs of Pre-Han China by Ssu-ma Ch'ien* (Bloomington & Indianapolis: Indiana University Press, 1994), pp. 21–2.

28 Legge, *Confucius*, p. 65, quoting from Sima Qian's *Shiji*, Chapter 63. For translation see Nienhauser, *The Grand Scribe's Records*, p. 22.

29 Yang and Yang, *Records of the Historian*, p. 3.

30 Legge, *Confucius*, pp. 67–8, referring to the *Narratives of the School*, vol. 4, and quoting *Liji*, II, Section II. iii. 10.

31 I have slightly changed Leys' translation here for clarity. See Leys, *The Analects*, 7.14, p. 30.

32 Yang and Yang, *Records of the Historian*, p. 3.

33 Legge, *Confucius*, p.68, quoting from the *Narratives of the School*, vol. II, Book 6.

34 Yang and Yang, *Records of the Historian*, p. 4.

35 Leys, *The Analects*, 13.3, p. 61.

36 Yang and Yang, *Records of the Historian*, p. 4.

37 Clements, *Confucius*, pp. 36–7, quoting from the *Kong Family Masters' Anthology*, II.14 (Ariel, Y., *Kung-ts'ung-tzu – The K'ung Family Masters' Anthology* [Princeton: Princeton University Press, 1989]. p. 85).

38 Yang and Yang, *Records of the Historian*, p. 4. It has been suggested that these criticisms of Confucius were not actually made by Yan Ying, who was very similar to Confucius in many ways, but by other statesmen in Qi who were suspicious of Confucius and his attachment to ritual, ceremonies and the ways of the ancients. See Legge, *Confucius*, p. 69.

39   Yang and Yang, *Records of the Historian*, p. 4.

40   Clements, *Confucius*, pp. 41–2, drawing from the *Kong Family Masters' Anthology*, II, 14 (Ariel, p. 77).

Chapter 5: Return to Lu

1   Leys, *The Analects*, 3.6, pp. 10–11.

2   Leys, *The Analects*, 3.1, p. 10.

3   Leys, *The Analects*, 3.2, p. 10.

4   Legge, *Confucius*, notes p. 317.

5   Leys, *The Analects*, 17.1, p. 85.

6   Leys, *The Analects*, 17.5, p. 86.

7   The final flight of Gongshan Furao and Yang Hu may not have been until 498 BC, when the Duke had regained some power over the Three Families and Confucius was employed by him as Minister of Justice. Annping Chin notes that Gongshan Furao (aka Gongshan Buniu) maintained control of Bi until 498, when Confucius attempted to dismantle the strongholds of the Three Families in order to empower Duke Ding. Just as the Duke and his forces were preparing to attack Bi, Gongshan and his Jisun forces attacked the capital, and the Duke and his family hid in a palace tower. It was Confucius who ordered officers to lead an assault on the Jisun troops, defeating them, and 'the two rebel leaders ran for the state of Qi'. Chin, Annping, *The Authentic Confucius*, p. 30.

8   Leys, *The Analects*, 2.4, p. 6.

9   Leys, *The Analects*, 9.23, p. 42.

10   Leys, *The Analects*, 17.26, p. 71.

11   Clements, *Confucius*, Chronology, p. xiv.

12   Baber, Ray Erwin, 'Marriage in Ancient China', *Journal of Educational Sociology*, vol. 8 (American Sociological Association, November 1934), pp. 139–49.

13   Leys, *The Analects*, 8.13, p. 37.

14   Yang and Yang, *Records of the Historian*, p. 6.

15   *The Book of Changes* is a text that is also closely identified with
     Daoism, and contains an ancient system of cosmology and
     philosophy that uses symbols to find order in chance events. *The
     Spring and Autumn Annals* is a history of the state of Lu from 722
     to 479 BC that has also traditionally been attributed to Confucius.
     The Book of Music is sometimes considered the Sixth Classic, but
     became a chapter in *The Book of Rites*. As well as the Five
     Confucian Classics, followers of Confucianism also extol the Four
     Books of Song Dynasty Neo-Confucianist Zhu Xi – *The Analects
     (Lunyu)*, *The Great Learning (Do Xue)*, *The Doctrine of the Mean
     (Zhongyong)*, and *Mencius (Mengzi)*, the first three of which have
     also traditionally been attributed in some form to Confucius.

16   Yang and Yang, *Records of the Historian*, p. 6.

17   Leys, *The Analects*, 14.26, p. 70.

18   Leys, *The Analects*, 2.4, p. 6.

19   Leys, *The Analects*, 13.10, p. 62.

20   Leys, *The Analects*, 2.1, p. 6.

21   Legge, *Confucius*, p. 72, citing *Narratives of the School*, Book I

22   Yang and Yang, *Records of the Historian*, p. 6.

23   Legge, *Confucius*, p. 73, citing *Narratives of the School*, Book I.
     Legge says that Confucius told the Jisun leader that he united the
     tombs to 'hide his disloyalty', while Clements, who also cites this
     episode from Legge, writes that Confucius claimed to be 'atoning
     for his disloyalty to his former master' (Clements, *Confucius*,
     p. 71). The latter seems a more plausible explanation.

24   It is not clear exactly when Confucius was promoted from
     Minister of Works to Minister of Justice and what his
     achievements were in each post. Sima Qian simply states, 'He was
     promoted to be Minister of Works, then Chief Justice', and then
     goes on to recount Confucius' successful work in diplomacy at
     Jiagu in the tenth year of Duke Ding's reign, namely 500 BC (Yang
     and Yang, *Records of the Historian*, p. 6). Legge follows Sima
     Qian's vague chronology (Legge, *Confucius*, pp. 72–3) but
     mentions Confucius' issue with Duke Zhao's tomb after stating

that he became Chief Justice. Clements chooses to attribute both the episode with Duke Zhao's tomb and his diplomatic coup at Jiagu to his time as Minister of Works (Clements, *Confucius*, pp. 70–71). While the interment of Duke Zhao might indeed have been one of the duties of a Minister of Works, it seems to this author more likely that he would have joined an important political summit with the Duke in the role of Minister of Justice.

25 Yang and Yang, *Records of the Historian*, pp. 6–7.

26 Yang and Yang, *Records of the Historian*, p. 7. The term 'barbarian' is a translation of the Chinese words *yi* or *di*, which refer to the non-Chinese peoples of the east and north of China, who were considered by the Zhou Chinese to be non-cultured foreigners.

27 Yang and Yang, *Records of the Historian*, p. 7.

28 This version of the story follows Legge's account of the summit meeting, which presents the Duke's offer to provide entertainment as a celebration after signing the treaty (see Legge, *Confucius*, pp. 73–4). Legge's account is based on that given in the *Zuo Zhuan* commentary of *The Spring and Autumn Annals*, Duke Ding, tenth year. Sima Qian records that the Duke of Qi proposed the entertainment after the dismissal of the barbarians, and then, once Confucius had refused the entertainment (and ordered the performers killed for 'beguiling their lords'!), Duke Jing shame-facedly agreed to Lu's demands to return the territory taken from Lu (See Yang and Yang, *Records of the Historian*, p. 7.)

29 Legge, *Confucius*, p. 74, citing *Narratives of the School*, Book II. Here, we see an example of Confucius practising the principle that princes should behave like princes and fathers should behave like fathers, a notion that is closely connected with his doctrine of the 'Rectification of Names', in which language must be used correctly. As Minister of Justice, Confucius argued that it was not fair to punish a son for not being son-like if his father had not been father-like towards him. This doctrine was not simply meant to maintain a strict social hierarchy but to prevent those with power from abusing it and protect the weak from being abused.

30 Leys, *The Analects*, 13.11, 13.12, p. 62.

31 Yang and Yang, *Records of the Historian*, p. 8.

32 Yang and Yang, *Records of the Historian*, p. 8.

33 Yang and Yang, *Records of the Historian*, p. 8.

34 As Legge suggests, the position he was given was more likely that of 'chief minister' at specific ceremonies, such as the summit meeting in Jiagu (see Legge, *Confucius*, p. 74, note 2). This position still, however, gave him a considerable amount of influence over the Duke and his policies.

35 Yang and Yang, *Records of the Historian*, p. 8, and Legge, *Confucius*, p. 75, citing *Narratives of the School*, Book II.

36 Yang and Yang, *Records of the Historian*, p. 9, and Legge, *Confucius*, pp. 75–6.

Chapter 6: Confucius' Followers

1 Nienhauser, *The Grand Scribe's Records*, vol. 7, p. 63.

2 The full list is as follows. Virtue: Yan Hui, Min Ziqian, Ran Boniu, Ran Yong. Eloquence: Zai Yu, Zigong. Government: Ran Qiu, Zilu. Culture: Ziyou, Zixia. See Leys, *The Analects*, 11.3, p. 49.

3 Legge, *Confucius*, p. 115.

4 Leys, *The Analects*, 12.12, p. 57.

5 Nienhauser, *The Grand Scribe's Records*, vol. 7, p. 68.

6 Leys, *The Analects*, 7.11, p. 30.

7 Nienhauser, *The Grand Scribe's Records*, vol. 7, p. 67.

8 Nienhauser, *The Grand Scribe's Records*, vol. 7, p. 67.

9 Leys, *The Analects*, 11.12, p. 50.

10 Leys, *The Analects*, 9.12, p. 41.

11 Leys, *The Analects*, 5.7, p. 20.

12 Leys, *The Analects*, 9.27, pp. 42–43.

13 Leys, *The Analects*, 17.7, p. 86.

14 Chin, *The Authentic Confucius*, p. 91 and notes p. 233 citing, scholar Qian Mu's argument that he sought Nanzi's influence.

15   Yang and Yang, *Records of the Historian*, p. 10.

16   Leys, *The Analects*, 6.28, p. 27.

17   Nienhauser, *The Grand Scribe's Records*, vol. 7, p. 70.

18   Leys, *The Analects*, 1.15, p. 5.

19   Chin, *The Authentic Confucius*, p. 64.

20   Leys, *The Analects*, 5.9, p. 20.

21   Leys, *The Analects*, 5.4. p. 19.

22   It seems highly unlikely that Confucius would have been impressed by Zigong's financial success, as he considered the cultivation of the self to be more important than the cultivation of wealth. To Confucius, 'A gentleman seeks the Way, he does not seek a living' (Leys, *The Analects*, 15.32, p. 78). Over the centuries, followers of Confucius, especially Mencius, expressed a strong distaste for merchants and profit, as they believed that the desire for financial gain was antithetical to the desire to follow the Way.

23   These references to Zigong's life and character are described by Sima Qian in Chapter VII of his history of Pre-Han China, which is devoted to Confucius' disciples. See Nienhauser, *The Grand Scribe's Records*, vol. 7, p. 70–74.

24   Nienhauser, *The Grand Scribe's Records*, vol. 7, p. 69.

25   *The Analects*, 6.26, as translated in Chin, *The Authentic Confucius*, p. 67.

26   Leys, *The Analects*, 5.10, p. 20.

27   Leys, *The Analects*, 17.21, pp. 88–9.

28   Leys, *The Analects*, 16.1, p. 80.

29   Leys, *The Analects*, 6.4, pp. 24–5.

30   Leys, *The Analects*, 11.17, p. 51.

31   Chin, *The Authentic Confucius*, p. 84.

32   Nienhauser, *The Grand Scribe's Records*, vol. 7, p. 64, Sima Qian quotes *The Analects*, 6.11.

33   Nienhauser, *The Grand Scribe's Records*, vol. 7, p. 64, Sima Qian quotes *The Analects*, 2.9.

34   Leys, *The Analects*, 6.7, p. 25.

35   Leys, *The Analects*, 12.1, p. 55.

36   Leys, *The Analects*, 9.11, p. 41.
37   Leys, *The Analects*, 9.21, p. 42.
38   Leys, *The Analects*, 5.5, p. 19.
39   Nienhauser, *The Grand Scribe's Records*, vol. 7, p. 66, Sima Qian quotes *The Analects*, 6.1.
40   Nienhauser, *The Grand Scribe's Records*, vol. 7, p. 66, Sima Qian quotes *The Analects*, 6.6.
41   See Note 1.
42   Nienhauser, *The Grand Scribe's Records* vol. 7, p. 65.
43   Nienhauser, *The Grand Scribe's Records*, vol. 7, p. 65, Sima Qian quotes *The Analects*, 6.10. See also Leys, *The Analects*, 6.10, p. 25 and notes p. 147.

Chapter 7: The Wandering Years

1   Legge, *Confucius*, p. 76, quoting *The Analects*, 3.24.
2   Annping Chin suggests that the border warden's words may have been a sort of prophecy, a message to Confucius that it was Heaven's wish for him to travel the empire rousing people – like the ringer of a bell – to follow a more righteous path. Since he was destined to be a teacher and not a government official, he should not therefore be worried about not attaining a government office. See Chin, *The Authentic Confucius*, p. 92.
3   Leys, *The Analects*, 13.7, p. 61.
4   Leys, *The Analects*, 14.19, p. 69.
5   Yang and Yang, *Records of the Historian*, p. 10. According to Sima Qian's account of Confucius' wanderings, the teacher and his group travelled thousands of miles, staying in a total of seven different states, and moved back and forth between states several times. Annping Chin notes that the philosopher Zhuangzi, who lived 200 years earlier than Sima Qian, recorded a much simpler journey, with the group only staying in four states: Wei, Song, Chen and Cai. She maps out his possible itinerary as follows:

'Confucius started out in Wei, went through Song to Chen and Cai and possibly to Chu (to the district of She, which is mentioned in *The Analects*), and, on his way back, stopped by Chen and spent a few more years in Wei before returning to Lu.' Sima Qian's account, on which this chapter is primarily based, depicts Confucius moving back and forth between states, for example staying in the state of Wei on at least three separate occasions. Such a chaotic journey, in which Confucius is depicted as a restless soul who cannot decide where to live, may have been described as such by Sima Qian to lend drama to his account of Confucius' life (see Chin, *The Authentic Confucius*, p. 86).

6   Yang and Yang, *Records of the Historian*, p. 10. Although Yan Hui made this famous declaration of devotion to Confucius, he died a few months before Confucius' own death. Yan Hui's death was devastating to Confucius, in part because of his fondness for the young man, but also because Confucius saw in him great spiritual and moral potential that would not now realised.

7   Yang and Yang, *Records of the Historian*, p. 10.

8   Yang and Yang, *Records of the Historian*, pp. 10–11.

9   Legge, *Confucius*, p. 78, citing *The Analects*, 9.18.

10   Leys, *The Analects*, 11.26, p. 53.

11   Leys, *The Analects*, notes pp. 173–4.

12   Yang and Yang, *Records of the Historian*, p. 11.

13   Ching, Annping, *Confucius*, p. 102.

14   Clements, *Confucius*, pp. 93–94.

15   Yang and Yang, *Records of the Historian*, p. 11. It should be noted that physiognomy has been an important science in China from before Confucius' time. According to its practitioners, one's facial features reveal one's character and one's fate, so the comparison of Confucius' forehead, neck and shoulders with those of legendary heroes is significant. He had the features of someone great, yet he appeared as bedraggled as a stray dog.

16   Yang and Yang, *Records of the Historian*, p. 11.

17   Yang and Yang translate the Chinese term Nuzhen as Churchen

(Jurchen) (*Records of the Historian*, pp. 11–12). This is a mistranslation. The Sushen and Jurchen, while inhabiting a similar region in the north, were separated by more than a thousand years. There is no evidence that they are related. (Conversation with Jonathan Markley, March 2009.)

18 Yang and Yang, *Records of the Historian*, pp. 11–12.

19 Clements, *Confucius*, p. 95.

20 Yang and Yang, *Records of the Historian*, p. 12.

21 Yang and Yang, *Records of the Historian*, p. 12.

22 Yang and Yang, *Records of the Historian*, p. 13.

23 Leys, *The Analects*, 17.7, p. 86, and Yang and Yang, *Records of the Historian*, p. 13.

24 Yang and Yang, *Records of the Historian*, pp. 13–14.

25 Yang and Yang, *Records of the Historian*, p. 14.

26 There is some disagreement about the timing of Ran Qiu's appointment. Some scholars have him leaving Confucius and returning to Lu three to four years into his wandering period. I am following Siam Qian's account here, which places Ran Qiu's departure a few years later. See Yang and Yang, *Records of the Historian*, p. 15.

27 Yang and Yang, *Records of the Historian*, p. 16.

28 Leys, *The Analects*, 13.18, p. 63.

29 The case was also cited by Han Feizi (d. 233 BC), a Legalist thinker of the Qin dynasty, who, in his discussions of the inconsistencies within different social relationships and the need for laws to control society, pointed out the paradox that a man like Upright Gong could at once be 'honest in the service of his sovereign but a villain to his own father'. See de Bary, William Theodore (general editor), *Sources of Chinese Tradition*, vol. 1 (New York: Columbia University Press, 1960, rev. 1999), p. 201.

30 Yang and Yang, *Records of the Historian*, p. 16.

31 Yang and Yang, *Records of the Historian*, pp. 16–17.

32 Yang and Yang, *Records of the Historian*, p. 17.

33 Annping Chin points out that it was very unlikely that the men of

Cai and Chen would have worked together to stop Confucius reaching Chu, as they were themselves enemies. She suggests it is more likely that Confucius and his followers simply became lost in the wilderness and had no plan to fall back on in case of trouble. To Sima Qian, a jealous enemy forcing Confucius into adverse circumstances made for a more exciting story than a lost group of travellers (see Chin, *The Authentic Confucius*, p. 108).

34 Yang and Yang, *Records of the Historian*, p. 19.
35 Yang and Yang, *Records of the Historian*, pp. 20–21.
36 Chin, *The Authentic Confucius*, p. 92, citing Mencius 3B:3, from *Mengzi Zhengyi*, pp. 247–51.

Chapter 8: The Final Years

1   Chin, The *Authentic Confucius*, p. 123.
2   Yang and Yang, *Records of the Historian*, p. 21.
3   Yang and Yang, *Records of the Historian*, p. 21.
4   Yang and Yang, *Records of the Historian*, p. 21.
5   Leys, *The Analects*, 12.19, p. 58.
6   Chin, *The Authentic Confucius*, pp. 125–6.
7   Leys, *The Analects*, 11.17, p. 51.
8   Chin, *The Authentic Confucius*, p. 130.
9   Chin, *The Authentic Confucius*, p. 130.
10 Leys, *The Analects*, 12.6, p. 56.
11 Leys, *The Analects*, 12.10, p. 57.
12 Leys, *The Analects*, 2.18, p. 8.
13 Leys, *The Analects*, 15.6, pp. 74–5. It should be noted that, according to Sima Qian, this exchange happened while Confucius was travelling between Chen and Cai and Zizhang was with him, suggesting that he may have been a student before Confucius' return to Lu. See Nienhauser, *The Grand Scribe's Records*, p. 75.
14 Leys, *The Analects*, 11.3, p. 49.
15 Leys, *The Analects*, 13.17, p. 63.

16 Leys, *The Analects*, 3.8, p. 11. Note that Confucius had a similar discussion with an older student, Zigong, about a poem in *The Book of Songs* and paid Zigong a similar compliment. See Leys, *The Analects*, 1.15, p. 5.

17 In the same chapter of *The Analects*, two verses quote Zizhang regarding virtue and morality (19.1, 19.2), while one (19.3) describes a disagreement between Zizhang and Zixia about Confucius' teachings on friendship and social intercourse.

18 Leys, *The Analects*, 11.16, p. 51.

19 Yang and Yang, *Records of the Historian*, pp. 21–2.

20 For a fuller discussion of the role of Confucius in the creation of China's literary classics, see Li Sijing, *Sources of the Confucian Tradition: The Five Classics and the Four Books* (Jinn: Shandong Friendship Press, 1998).

21 Yang and Yang, *Records of the Historian*, p. 25.

22 Yang and Yang, *Records of the Historian*, p. 25.

23 Yang and Yang, *Records of the Historian*, p. 22. The earliest Chinese books were scrolls resembling modern rattan placemats. They were made out of vertical bamboo or wooden strips that were bound together with thongs; Chinese characters were written vertically, from top to bottom and from right to left. These books were unrolled for reading and then rolled up again for storage.

24 For more on Confucius and these early texts, see Loewe, Michael (editor), *Early Chinese Texts: A Bibliographical Guide* (Berkeley: University of California, Berkeley, 1993).

25 Yang and Yang, *Records of the Historian*, p. 23.

26 Leys, *The Analects*, 6.22, p. 27.

27 Yang and Yang, *Records of the Historian*, p. 23.

28 Clements, *Confucius*, pp. 105–6, from Shaughnessy, E., *I Ching: The Classic of Changes* (New York: Ballantine, 1996) p. 238.

29 Yang and Yang, *Records of the Historian*, p. 24.

30 Yang and Yang, *Records of the Historian*, p. 23.

31 Leys, *The Analects*, 10.19, p. 47.

32 Clements, *Confucius*, p. 109, from Chen, K. and Hu Zhihui (editors), *Zuo's Commentary* (Changsha, Hunan People's Press, 1997).

33 Leys, *The Analects*, 5.9, p. 20.

34 Leys, *The Analects*, 11.9, p. 50.

35 Sima Qian records Yan Hui's death before the sighting of the *qilin*, so the symbolism of the creature is even more poignant for him, as he felt he had no successor. See Yang and Yang, *Records of the Historian*, p. 24.

36 Leys, *The Analects*, 11.10, p. 50.

37 Leys, *The Analects*, 11.11, p. 50.

38 Yang and Yang, *Records of the Historian*, p. 25.

39 Legge, *Confucius*, p. 87, quoting the *Liji*, II, Section I.ii, 20.

40 Yang and Yang, *Records of the Historian*, p. 26.

Conclusion:
The Legacy of Confucius and His Teachings

1 Leys, *The Analects*, 15.20, p. 76.

2 For a fascinating exploration of this issue, see Fingarette, Herbert, *Confucius: The Secular as Sacred* (Prospect Heights, Illinois: Waveland Press, Inc., 1972).

3 Although I agree that Confucianism has characteristics both of a religion and a political ideology, I am more comfortable with the term 'philosophy' when referring to it. For the sake of simplicity, I will refer to Confucianism as a philosophy throughout this chapter.

4 Waley, Arthur, *Three Ways of Thought in Ancient China* (Stanford: Stanford University Press, 1982), p. 83.

5 De Bary, *Sources of Chinese Tradition*, p. 92.

6 De Bary, *Sources of Chinese Tradition*, p. 94, quoting from the *Mencius*, I A:3, I A:7 and VII A:22.

7 De Bary, *Sources of Chinese Tradition*, p. 104, quoting from the *Xunzi*, Chapter 23.

8   De Bary, *Sources of Chinese Tradition*, p. 141, citing Sima Qian, 6:23b or for a counterbalance to Sima Qian's account of the Confucian martyrs under the First Emperor, see Ulrich Neininger, 'Burning the Scholars: on the origin of a Confucian martyrs legend' in Wolfram Eberhard, Krzystof Gawlikowski and Carl Albrecht Seyschab (eds.) *East Asian Civilisation: new attempts at understanding traditions (2) Nation and Mythology*, n.p., Simon and Magiera, 1983

9   De Bary, *Sources of Chinese Tradition*, p. 146.

10   Loewe, Michael, *Ways to Paradise: The Chinese Quest for Immortality* (Taipei: SMC Publishing Inc., 1979), p. 3.

11   Not all Han dynasty Confucianists believed in the synthesis of Daoist beliefs in *yin* and *yang* and the Five Elements with the teachings of Confucius. Those who did were part of what was known as the New Text School, in part because they based their understanding of Confucius' teachings on early Han dynasty texts written in a new script developed in the Qin dynasty. Those Han Confucianists who opposed what they considered to be the superstition and supernaturalism of the New Text School formed the Old Text School, which looked to surviving Zhou dynasty texts written in ancient script as a source of the true teachings of Confucius.

12   Loewe, *Ways to Paradise*, pp. 7–8.

13   De Bary, *Sources of Chinese Tradition*, p. 369.

14   De Bary, *Sources of Chinese Tradition*, p. 491.

15   For a discussion of the impact of Neo-Confucianism on Chinese government and culture from the twelfth to seventeenth centuries, see Bol, Peter K., *Neo-Confucianism in History* (Cambridge: Harvard University Asia Center [East Asian Monographs], 2008).

16   Ebrey, Patricia Buckley, Walthall, Anne, Palais, James B., *East Asia: A Cultural, Social, and Political History* (Boston: Houghton Mifflin Company, 2006) pp. 281–2.

17   For an examination of the work of Qing Evidential Research

scholars, see Elman, Benjamin A., *From Philosophy to Philology: Intellectual and Social Aspects of Change in Late Imperial China* (Los Angeles: UCLA Asia Institute [Asian Pacific Monographs series], 2001).

18 See Ambrose Y.C. King's chapter, 'State Confucianism and Its Transformation: The Restructuring of the State-Society in Taiwan', in Tu Wei-Ming (editor), *Confucian Traditions in East Asian Modernity: Moral Education and Economic Culture in Japan and the Four Mini-Dragons* (Cambridge, Massachusetts and London, England: Harvard University Press/American Academy of Arts and Sciences, 1996).

19 Koh Byong-ik, 'Confucianism in Contemporary Korea', in Tu Wei-Ming, *Confucian Traditions in East Asian Modernity*, p. 191.

20 Eckert, Carter J. et al., *Korea Old and New: A History* (Seoul: Ilchokak Publishers/Cambridge, Korea Institute, Harvard University, 1990), p. 37.

21 Eckert, *Korea Old and New: A History*, p. 64.

22 Eckert, *Korea Old and New: A History*, p. 73.

23 See Connor, Mary E. (editor), *The Koreas* (Santa Barbara, CA: ABC-CLIO Publishers, 2009), Chapter 5 (c): 'Women and Marriage', pp. 197–9.

24 Koh Byong-ik, 'Confucianism in Contemporary Korea', in Tu Wei-Ming, *Confucian Traditions in East Asian Modernity*, p. 192.

25 Connor, *The Koreas*, Chapter 5: 'Religion and Thought', p. 175.

26 Nosco, Peter (editor), *Confucianism and Tokugawa Culture* (Honolulu: University of Hawai'i Press, 1997), p. 5.

27 De Bary, William Theodore, *Sources of Japanese Tradition*, vol. 1 (New York: Columbia University Press, 1958).

28 Kasulis, Thomas P. (1998), 'Japanese Philosophy', in C. Craig (editor), *Routledge Encyclopedia of Philosophy* (London: Routledge, retrieved 29 April 2009 from http://www.rep.routledge.com/article/G100SECT2).

29 De Bary, *Sources of Japanese Tradition*, p. 59.

30 Nosco, *Confucianism and Tokugawa Culture*, p. 6.

31 For more on the adoption of Neo-Confucianism in the early Tokugawa period, see Herbert Ooms' essay, 'Neo-Confucianism and the Formation of early Tokugawa Ideology: Contours of a Problem', in Nosco, *Confucianism and Tokugawa Culture*, Chapter 2.

32 Nosco, *Confucianism and Tokugawa Culture*, p. 10

33 Yamashita, Samuel Hideo, 'The Writings of Ogyu Sorai (1666–1728)', in Nosco, *Confucianism and Tokugawa Culture*, Chapter 6.

34 Cima, Ronald J. (editor), *Vietnam: A Country Study* (Washington: GPO for the Library of Congress, 1987, http://countrystudies.us/Vietnam/4.htm).

35 Cima, *Vietnam* (http://countrysides.us/vietnam/11.htm).

36 Edwards, Michael, *East-West Passage: The Travel of Ideas, Arts and Inventions between Asia and the Western World* (New York: Taplinger Publishing Company, 1971), p. 104.

37 Edwards, *East-West Passage*, p. 105.

38 http://www.humorsphere.com/confucius/confucious_sayings.htm (note the misspelling of Confucius' name).

39 From CNN's *Anderson Cooper 360°*, *The Shot*, Tuesday 12 May 2009, http://www.cnn.com/video/?/video/bestoftv/2009/05/12/ac.shot.tue sday.cnn

Select Bibliography

Historical, social, religious and political background

Baber, Ray Erwin, 'Marriage in Ancient China', *Journal of Educational Sociology*, vol. 8, American Sociological Association, 3 November 1934

De Bary, William Theodore, *Sources of Chinese Tradition*, vol. 1 (New York: Columbia University Press, 1960, revised 1999)

Bol, Peter K., *Neo-Confucianism in History* (Cambridge: Harvard University Asia Center, East Asian Monographs, 2008)

Creel, Howard, *Chinese Thought: From Confucius to Mao Tse-Tung* (Chicago/London: Chicago University Press, 1953)

Dien, Albert, 'Chinese Beliefs in the Afterworld', in *The Quest for Eternity: Chinese Ceramic Sculptures from the People's Republic of China* (Los Angeles/San Francisco: Los Angeles County Museum of Art/Chronicle Books, 1987), pp. 1–15

Ebrey, Patricia Buckley, *Chinese Civilization: A Sourcebook* (New York: The Free Press, second edition, 1993)

Ebrey, Patricia Buckley, *The Cambridge Illustrated History of China* (Cambridge: Cambridge University Press, 1999)

Faulkenhausen, Lothar von, *Chinese Society in the Age of Confucius:*

The Archaeological Evidence (Los Angeles: Cotsen Institute of Archaeology, UCLA, 2006)

Goldin, Paul Rakita, *The Culture of Sex in Ancient China* (Honolulu: University of Hawai'i Press, 2002)

Lewis, Mark Edward, *The Construction of Space in Ancient China* (Albany: State University of New York, 2006)

Li, Chenyang (ed.), *The Sage and the Second Sex, Confucianism, Ethics, and Gender* (Chicago and La Salle, Illinois: Open Court, a division of Carus, 2000)

Loewe, Michael, *Ways to Paradise: The Chinese Quest for Immortality* (Taipei: SMC Publishing, 1979)

Waley, Arthur, *Three Ways of Thought in Ancient China* (Stanford: Stanford University Press, 1982)

Wang, Robin R. (ed.), *Images of Women in Chinese Thought and Culture: Writings from the Pre-Qin Period through the Song Dynasty* (Indianapolis: Hackett Publishing Co., 2003)

Biographies and commentaries on Confucius

Burgan, Michael, *Confucius: Chinese Philosopher and Teacher*, Signature Lives series (for younger readers) (Minneapolis: Compass Books, 2009)

Chin, Annping, *The Authentic Confucius: A Life of Thought and Politics* (New York: Scribner, 2007)

Clements, Jonathan, *Confucius: A Biography* (Stroud: Sutton Publishing, 2004)

Do-Dinh, Pierre (trans. Charles Lam Markmann), *Confucius and Chinese Humanism* (New York: Funk & Wagnalls, 1969)

Fingarette, Herbert, *Confucius: The Secular as Sacred* (Prospect Heights, Illinois: Waveland Press, 1972)

Nienhauser, William H. Jr. (ed.), Tsai-fa Cheng, Zhongli Lu, William H. Nienhauser Jr. and Robert Reynolds (trans.), *The Grand Scribe's Records*, vol. 8, *Memoirs of Pre-Han China by Ssu-ma Ch'ien* (Bloomington and Indianapolis: Indiana University Press, 1994)

Wilhelm, Richard, *Confucius and Confucianism* (New York: Harcourt Brace Jovanovitch, 1931)

Yang, Hsien-yi and Gladys Yang (trans. and eds), *Selections from Records of the Historian by Szuma Chien* (Beijing: Foreign Languages Press, 1979)

Versions of The Analects

Lau, D.C., *Confucius: The Analects* (London: Penguin Books, 1979)

Legge, James, *Confucius: Confucian Analects, The Great Learning and The Doctrine of the Mean* (Oxford: Clarendon Press, 1893–5. Reprint, Mineola, New York: Dover, 1971)

Leys, Simon, *The Analects of Confucius* (New York: W.W. Norton, 1997)

Waley, Arthur, *The Analects of Confucius* (New York: Vintage Books, 1989. Original edition New York: Macmillan, 1938)

General

Armstrong, Karen, *The Great Transformation: The Beginning of Our Religious Traditions* (New York: Anchor Books, 2006)

De Bary, William Theodore, *Sources of Japanese Tradition*, vol. 1 (New York: Columbia University Press, 1958)

Cima, Ronald J. (ed.), *Vietnam: A Country Study* (Washington: GPO for the Library of Congress, 1987; http://countrystudies.us/vietnam/4.htm)

Connor, Mary E. (ed.), *The Koreas* (Santa Barbara, CA: ABC-CLIO Publishers, 2009)

Ebrey, Patricia Buckley, Walthall, Anne and Palais, James B., *East Asia: A Cultural, Social, and Political History* (Boston: Houghton Mifflin, 2006)

Edwards, Michael, *East-West Passage: The Travel of Ideas, Arts and Inventions between Asia and the Western World* (New York: Taplinger Publishing Company, 1971)

Elman, Benjamin A., *From Philosophy to Philology: Intellectual and Social Aspects of Change in Late Imperial China* (Los Angeles: UCLA Asia Institute, Asian Pacific Monographs series, 2001)

Korea Old and New: A History (Seoul: Ilchokak Publishers/ Cambridge, Korea Institute, Harvard University, 1990)

Liu, Chen (ed.), (trans. He Zhaoshu), *Confucius Temple, Mansion and Family Cemetery*, World Cultural and National Heritage (China Volume) (Beijing: China Intercontinental Press, 2002)

Loewe, Michael (ed.), *Early Chinese Texts: A Bibliographical Guide* (Berkeley: University of California, Berkeley, 1993)

Nosco, Peter (ed.), *Confucianism and Tokugawa Culture* (Honolulu: University of Hawai'i Press, 1997)

Tu, Wei-Ming (ed.), *Confucian Traditions in East Asian Modernity: Moral Education and Economic Culture in Japan and the Four Mini-Dragons* (Cambridge, Massachusetts, and London: Harvard University Press/American Academy of Arts and Sciences, 1996)

Waley, Arthur (trans.), *The Book of Songs: The Ancient Chinese Classic of Poetry* (New York: Grove Press, 1996)

Index